Populisms. A Quick Immersion

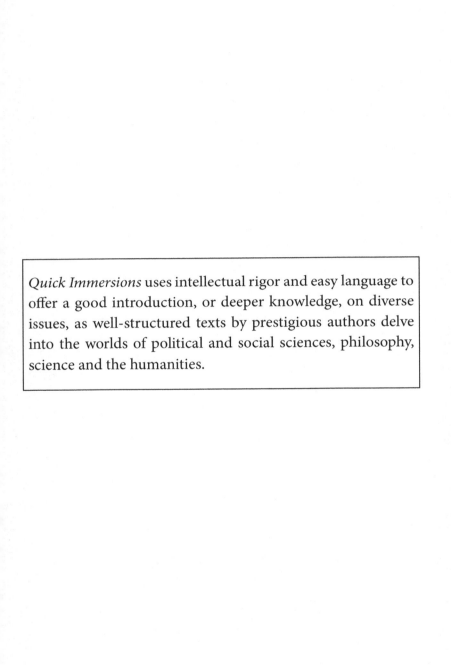

Quick Immersions uses intellectual rigor and easy language to offer a good introduction, or deeper knowledge, on diverse issues, as well-structured texts by prestigious authors delve into the worlds of political and social sciences, philosophy, science and the humanities.

Carlos de la Torre

POPULISMS
A Quick Immersion

Tibidabo Publishing

Copyediting by Lori Gerson
Cover art by Raimon Guirado
For photograph credits, please see page 7.

First published 2019

Visit our Series on our Web:
www.quickimmersions.com

ISBN: 978-1-949845-01-3
1 2 3 4 5 6 7 8 9 10

Printed in the United States of America.

Contents

List of illustrations, tables and graphics   7

Introduction   9

1 What Populism is and How to Study it   23

2 Populist Leadership   65

3 How Leaders are Linked with their Followers   100

4 The Promises and Perils of Populism
for Democracy   128

Conclusions   172

Further Reading   185

List of illustrations, tables and graphics

1. Populism. A word in a dictionary?   24
©Agata Gładykowska/123RF.COM

2. Image that symbolizes the networks of globalization.
Some authors attribute the rise in populisms to the
uncertainty and loss that structural changes brought
on by globalization have created in certain sectors
of the population.   41
©Nakit Jaroonsrirak/123RF.COM

3. Sculptural image of Human Rights. Paris, France.   53
©Gilles DeCruyenaere/123RF.COM

4. Occupy Wall Street was a popular insurgency
without clear leadership, inspired by the
15M movement in Spain. Its objective was
to continually occupy Wall Street, the financial
district in New York, as a protest against
the insecurity created by the global economic crisis.   67
©Aloysius Patrimonio/123RF.COM

5. Group of Donald Trump supporters on the
USS Iowa battleship in San Pedro, California,
adapting the slogan "Make American Great Again,"
which Trump used to seduce his followers
in the 2016 presidential campaign.   79
©Visions Of America LLC/123RF.COM

6. Crowds celebrate Macron's victory over
Marine Le Pen at the Louvre Museum after
the presidential elections. Paris (France), May 7, 2017.
©Grosescu Alberto/123RF.COM   84

7. Stamp printed in Argentina reflecting the myth
of Eva Peron devoted to her people.   113
©neftali77/123RF.COM

8. The famous Plaza de Mayo in Buenos Aires
(Argentina), recurrent setting for the affirmation
of rights.   135
©Adrian Wojcik/123RF.COM

9. Election posters from the Politicians for Syriza
campaign, January 28, 2015, Athens (Greece):
Portrait of Alexis Tsipras and the slogan
"Hope is on the way."   143
©sirylok/123RF.COM

10. Wood homes in a poor neighborhood
in Caracas, Venezuela.   147
©Kirill Zdorov/123RF.COM

11. Group of Bolivian women wearing their
traditional dress during the May 1 parade
in La Paz, Bolivia.   157
©Diego Grandi/123RF.COM

12. Poster in a bar in El Salvador supporting
Hugo Chávez. With varying levels of success,
Chávez promoted presidential candidates
in Peru, Nicaragua, Bolivia, Mexico and Ecuador.   181
©Matyas Rehak /123RF.COM

Table 1. Constructing the people   63
©Tibidabo Ediciones, SA

Introduction

Populism is no longer confined to Latin America, Asia, Africa or the Middle East. Nor is it at the margins of consolidated democracies. Nowadays, populists are in power in the U.S., Italy, Poland, Greece and Hungary. Some scholars see in populism the potential for a renewal of democracy and an alternative to the surrender of politics to technocrats. Yet most scholars are rightly concerned that populism could lead to the "disfigurement of democracy" as Nadia Urbinati puts it, or even worse to competitive authoritarianism. Some see strong Western institutions as shields to populist authoritarianism, while others are afraid that institutions on their own cannot protect democracy.

In the name of giving power back to the people, populists are challenging liberal constitutional practices and institutions. Citizens, scholars and journalists are again debating the relationships between democracy, populism and autocracy. They are asking questions such as: What are the differences and similarities between fascism and populism? When do populists become dictators? Others are arguing that because populism is inevitable, the left should construct progressive and non-racist narratives of the people to stop rightwing xenophobic populists.

The surge of populism globally has led to the publication of numerous books and academic articles. The editors of the *Oxford Handbook of Populism* note that between 1990 and 2010 approximately twelve-hundred books on populism were published in English. Major editorial houses like Routledge and Oxford published short introductory volumes, as well as comprehensive handbooks. Why should we bother reading yet another brief volume?

First, because most books, even those that have a comparative perspective, continue to focus on the U.S. and Europe, relegating Latin America and other experiences of the global south to marginal footnotes. This is partially explained by the Eurocentric biases of global academia. Yet Eurocentrism is not an excuse for sloppy scholarship. If researchers are interested in populism in power and as regimes, they should engage with the world regions where populism has not only challenged elites but also conquered power and governed. This book reverses the trend of most scholarship by analyzing populism globally and through the lense of Latin America. As historian Federico Finchelstein notes in *From Fascism to Populism in History*, populist regimes emerged with general Juan Perón in the 1940s when fascism was adapted to democratic times. Like the fascists, Peronists considered the people as a single entity that could be embodied in a leader, and viewed rivals as enemies. Yet in contrast to fascists, who abolished elections, the vote became the only legitimate tool for populists to get to power. Peronists and other populists attacked enemies at the rhetorical level, and unlike the fascists did not use paramilitary groups or widespread state repression to physically eliminate them. Unlike fascists, populists did not abolish democracy. Yet, as will be argued in this volume, the effects of populism on democracy depended on whether all the population was politically included in parties or not, the way in which the category of the people was articulated, the type of institutional system, and the nature of the crisis of political representation that led to its emergence.

By looking at populism globally, scholars can avoid the mistake of using colonial stereotypes as scholarship. For instance, in an otherwise excellent introductory volume, Cas Mudde and Cristóbal Rovira Kaltwasser argue that populist hyper-masculine leaders are more common in traditional societies with machismo cultures. Without denying that some leaders, such as Ecuadorian Abdalá Bucaram, talked about the size of his genitalia, macho discourse is not exclusively their backward cultural property. In societies that the authors of *Populism: A Very Short Introduction* label as having "more capitalist and materialist cultures," populists like Donald Trump also used vulgar tropes and misogynist discourses. A global and historical engagement with diverse populisms is a good antidote to cultural stereotypes.

When populism is analyzed globally, the novelty is not its presence in most world regions. After all, populists have challenged the power of political and economic elites since the nineteenth century, and the first self-described Populist Party was formed in the U.S. in 1891. What is new is that populists are in office not only in Venezuela, Bolivia, the Philippines or Turkey but also in the U.S. as well as in other consolidated Western liberal democracies. By learning from the experiences of populism in the global south, citizens, activists, journalists and politicians in the global north might avoid making the same mistakes when dealing with populists in power. For instance, the media in Venezuela and Ecuador played into the politics of confrontation by obsessively focusing on the shocking words and performances of Hugo Chávez or Rafael Correa. U.S. television is following the same path with its fixation on Trump's latest outrageous tweet. The media became a site of democratic resistance in Latin America when it uncovered, at great personal and institutional costs, cases of corruption and abuses of power.

Contrary to scholars who shy away from normative engagements with populism, this book evaluates it from the perspectives of radical democracy. Democracy, as Nadia Urbinati argues, is an institutional order based on both constitutional norms and institutions, and on pluralist and vibrant public spheres and forums where citizens engage and participate in politics. Liberal constitutional norms protect citizens from the power of the state, powerful corporations and majoritarian rule. Under liberal democracy there are checks and balances, and institutions that promote accountability as well as free elections. As Jürgen Habermas said, liberal rights are not constraints on the people's sovereignty; on the contrary, they are the condition of possibility for democratic rule. Democracy is also based on spaces where citizens can voice their opinions in the public sphere, and form organizations and associations in civil society. Populists rightly criticize the deficits of participation and representation of real existing democracies. Populists often point to problems and issues that other politicians overlook. They, for instance, politicize fears about the loss of national sovereignty and anger at socioeconomic and political exclusions. If populists are right in some of their criticism on the malfunctioning of democracy, their solutions are problematic. Populism can lead to processes of democratic disfigurement when the complexities of modern society are reduced to the struggle between two antagonistic camps, and when one part of the population claims to represent the population as a whole. Under these conditions opponents do not have institutional or normative spaces to articulate dissent, becoming the hideous oligarchy, or the antinational other.

This book distinguishes different types of populism. Some politicize fears of cosmopolitanism using race, ethnicity and culture to mark the boundaries of inclusion to the people and the nation.

Other populists give meanings to feelings and emotions of exclusion, and anger against economic and political elites that pretend that neoliberalism is the only technically acceptable economic policy. They show how neoliberalism is a political economy that benefits some groups and classes at the expense of others. Some populists believe in the power of the unregulated market, others use the state to regulate the market and even attempt to create a third way between capitalism and communism. Some populists like Trump, Rodrigo Duterte or Jair Bolsonaro in Brazil promise law and order, while Hugo Chávez and his fellow travelers of socialism in the twenty-first century promised more and better democracy. Whereas Trump's populism aims to recreate a nostalgic white, patriarchal and heterosexual America, Chávez's was forward-looking, aiming to transform politics, society, the economy and culture.

Despite their different constructs of who is "the people," and dissimilar politicizations of grievances and emotions, populists share a similar logic. Populists aim to rupture exclusionary institutional systems to give power back to the people. They face enemies, and not democratic rivals. They appeal to reason and emotion to reduce the complexities of politics to the struggle between two antagonistic camps. Regardless of its potential inclusionary promise, the *pars pro toto* dynamic of populism is inherently autocratic because a part of the population claims to be its whole, and pretends to rule in the name of all.

A leader is constructed as the true voice and the only representative of the "real people." Some populist leaders are represented as the saviors of their people. Other leaders become avatars of patriotism and claim to know how to make things right for their people. Without a leader considered to be out of the ordinary, social movements that use a populist rhetoric are not yet populists.

In the past, and with the exception of the U.S. Populist Party, the term populism was used by external observers and not by the movements or parties to whom this label was attached. Things are changing in the twenty-first century. Leftwing populist parties like Podemos in Spain or Jean-Luc Mélenchon, leader of La France Insoumise, describe themselves as populists and use Ernesto Laclau's theories to challenge the establishment. Right-wing populists such as Marine Le Pen and Mateo Salvini proudly describe themselves as populists. In the U.S., Steve Bannon claimed, "Trump is the leader of a populist uprising… What Trump represents is a restoration of a true American capitalism and a revolution against state-sponsored socialism. Elites have taken all the upside for themselves and pushed the downside to the working and middle-class Americans."

The term populism has positive connotations in the U.S. Criticizing candidate Donald Trump, president Barack Obama for example said, "I care about poor people who are working really hard and don't have a chance to advance…I suppose that makes me a populist." Therefore, it is not a surprise that many liberals and leftists reject using this term to describe a right-wing reactionary, xenophobic and misogynist millionaire like Donald Trump. Paul Krugman wrote on August 2, 2018, in the *New York Times* "Stop Calling Trump a Populist." Some American radical democrats like Laura Grattan in *Populism's Power* distinguishes "the cruel aspirations" of right-wing populism —which is fueled by resentment and displaces the people's aspiration to power by acclaiming the rule of demagogues— from what she theorizes as "aspirational democratic populism." This form of populism, illustrated by the everyday democratic practices of the Populist Party or Occupy Wall Street, "cultivate people's rebellious aspirations not only to share in power but to do so in pluralistic, egalitarian ways across established horizons that restrict democracy." Unfortunately, most experiences of populism in power, even when they were built on democratic promises, were based on the *pars pro toto* logic. A sector of the population claimed to be the only rightful and truthful people under the leadership of their liberator. Once in power, populists often closed democratic spaces to the opposition, transforming rivals into existential enemies and followers into unconditional devotees.

Contrary to U.S. views of populism as emancipatory, in Latin America and Europe the term is often used to brand politicians and their followers as irrational and dangerous. Andrés Manuel López

Obrador in Mexico or Pablo Iglesias, the leader of Podemos, are represented as inherent threats to democracy, when their projects aim to renew and deepen democracy.

Populists blur traditional left-right distinctions. The National Rally (formerly the National Front) proposes to use the state to regulate globalization, is xenophobic, constructing Muslim men as the antithesis to Western cultural values, proclaims to defend Muslim women from misogynistic Muslim men, defends gay rights and is hyper nationalist. Nicole Curato in the *Journal of Contemporary Asia* explains that Rodrigo Duterte, who describes himself as a socialist, had a first cabinet made up of people of all sorts of ideologies and backgrounds: "Mindanao elites, members of the left endorsed by the Communist Party of the Philippines-National Democratic Front, a military official known for crushing the communist insurgency and traditional politicians." Rafael Correa was a left neo-Keynesian who sought to put the state at the center of development. Yet he was also a practicing Catholic opposed to abortion, gay marriage and gender ideologies.

To complicate matters further, the concept of populism continues to be contested, and periodically some scholars propose getting rid of it altogether. They point out that it refers to both the left and the right, to inclusion and autocracy, to state-centered or market-oriented economic policies, and to historical and contemporary cases that are dissimilar. Yet despite the calls to abolish it, scholars continue to write conceptual and empirical studies of populism. In contrast to the cacophony of definitions over the recent past, a few theories that will be reviewed in Chapter One are often used nowadays. Positivist-oriented scholars seek to produce a minimum definition to accumulate knowledge. Others refuse to reduce complex phenomena like populism to a couple of sentences and continue to use accumulative theories to make sense of how populism is grounded in history and in particular political, economic and cultural milieus.

The main political and scholarly disagreements are on the relationships between democratization and populism. For Ernesto Laclau, his students and followers, left-wing populism is the alternative to closed administrative orders that depoliticize society and rely on the rule of technocrats. Their objective is to build a people without xenophobic tropes to rupture exclusionary systems. Other scholars argue that the historical record of populism in power is the transformation of failed democracies into hybrid regimes. Venezuela and Ecuador, for example, had crises of political representation, and Chávez and Correa moved democracy to the gray zone between democracy and dictatorship. Nicolás Maduro went one step further, displacing Venezuela's hybrid regime toward autocracy when he disregarded the most basic rules of fair elections, incarcerated opponents and had elections that took place without minimum guarantees for the opposition. Yet not all populists displaced democracy to the gray zone of hybridism. Alexis Tsipras, after winning a referendum against austerity, capitulated to the Troika and Syriza became a sort of social democratic party. Nestor and Cristina Kirchner were not committed, and not permitted, to bring a populist rupture in Argentina. A complex civil society and strong judiciary did not allow Cristina to change the constitution to seek another reelection. The effects of populism on democracy depend on whether the population is politically incorporated in political parties or not, on the strength of domestic civil societies and supranational organizations, and on the force of liberal constitutional institutions.

In order to disentangle the effects of populism on democratization, inclusion and democracy have to be differentiated. Some populisms are inclusionary as they redistribute income and wealth, carry on fundamental structural reforms, expand the franchise and reassert popular culture against the culture of foreign-inspired elites. Yet inclusion is not the same as building democratic institutions and political cultures. Even when populisms were inclusionary, a part of the population appropriated the right to talk on behalf of the whole; a leader was invested as the only truthful and authorized voice of the people, and supporters became loyal followers. Dissent became treason, and the political was reduced to Schmittian struggles between friend and enemy. The politics of confrontation and polarization led to the reduction of spaces for dialogue and compromise, politics resembled zero-sum games between two camps, and those who were neither fans nor foes of the populists were forced to choose sides. In these gargantuan confrontations, the rules of the democratic game were bent and civil society became uncivil and belligerent. For some, populist polarization was the desirable beginning for revolutionary ruptures. For others, it signaled the beginning of the end of democracy.

I grew up in Ecuador, a county polarized by populism since José María Velasco Ibarra dominated its politics from the 1930s to the 1970s. He was president five times, but alas only finished one term in office. My childhood memories are filled with reminiscences of the smell of tear gas and confrontations between Velasco's followers and foes. I have vivid memories of throngs stoning *Diario El Tiempo*, where my father was the editor-in-chief, and fears that he was going to end up in jail for voicing dissent to Velasco's self-coup in 1971. I experienced firsthand the intolerance of a populist when president Rafael Correa insulted me twice on his weekly TV and radio show, for an opinion piece and an interview. As with all of those who were branded as enemies of the president, the people and the nation, Correa showed my photo. I was fortunate that Correa did not use the legal system to sue me, as he did with journalists, political cartoonists and the owners of media venues.

I have been researching the ambiguities of populism for democratization since the early 1990s when I wrote my dissertation on Velasco Ibarra's populism. I did ethnographic studies on Abdalá Bucaram, who was in power for six months, and Rafael Correa, who dominated Ecuadorian politics for a decade. Then I focused on comparative studies of radical populism in Venezuela, Bolivia and Ecuador, and later on global populism, drawing on Latin American experiences to understand Trump, for example. I have illustrated how populism was an inclusionary revolt against oligarchic elites. I have also argued that populist followers are not irrational masses in a state of anomie who follow demagogues. Yet, simultaneously, I have maintained that populists transform rivals into enemies, that a leader acts as the embodiment of the people, that fundamental rights such as the right of free information and assembly are limited by populists, and that a political culture of confrontation and polarization becomes a hindrance to citizenship.

This book, written for the general public, draws on my scholarship and critical engagements with theoretical and empirical studies of populism globally. The book is divided into four chapters. The first critically discusses the theoretical and normative claims of the most influential approaches to populism. The second focuses on populist leadership and uses Weber to discuss the charismatic links between leaders and followers, and how followers build a politician into an extraordinary leader. If the second chapter focuses on the words and performances of leaders, the third looks at the politics of organized followers. It analyzes populist organizations and the different links between leaders and followers. The fourth chapter deals with the emancipatory promises of populism while seeking power, and their autocratic practices when in power and as regimes. Whereas when challenging power populists promise inclusion and even redemption, once in power they attempt to transform a diverse population into the image of the people that is held by the leader.

Chapter 1

What Populism is and How to Study it

This chapter discusses the most influential historical and social scientific approaches to populism. It analyzes how these perspectives study its emergence, its effects on democratization and the normative claims made to evaluate populism. It distinguishes mass society, discursive, political and ideational theories of populism.

Mass Society

Writing after the traumas of fascism, the first round of historians and social scientists of populism were suspicious of its democratic credentials. Notions of crises, of the irrational responses of the masses to stress, and manipulation in conditions of anomie were at the center of social scientific and historical scholarship. Analyzing McCarthyism, Talcott Parsons wrote: "it is a generalization well-established in social sciences that neither individuals nor societies can undergo major structural changes without the likelihood of producing a considerable element of 'irrational' behavior." The expected responses to the stress produced by major structural transformations were anxiety, aggression focused on what was felt to be the source of strain, and a desire to reestablish a fantasy where everything will be all right, preferably as it was before the disruptive situation.

1. Populism. A word in a dictionary?

Contrary to the prevailing view of the U.S. populist movement and party of the 1890s as being progressive and democratizing, historian Richard Hofstadter in *The Age of Reform* showed its ambiguities. He argued that populists "aimed at the remedy of genuine ills, combined with strong moral convictions and with the choice of hatred as a kind of creed." Populists imagined the populace as innocent, productive and victimized by predatory elites. Their views of politics, he claimed, "assumed a delusive simplicity." It was a Manichean and conspiratorial outlook that attributed "demonic qualities to their foes." Populism was the result of an agrarian crisis and a transitional stage in the history of agrarian capitalism. Populists aimed to restore a golden age and their utopia "was in the past and not in the future." Its base of support was those who had attained only a low level of education, whose access to information was poor, and who were so completely shut out from access to the centers of power that they felt themselves completely deprived of self-defense and subjected to unlimited manipulation by those who wielded power.

Even though Hofstadter asserted that the populist movement and party "was not an unambiguous forerunner of modern authoritarian movements," the paranoid style in American politics reappeared with McCarthyism and other forms of "crank" pseudo-conservatism. This opinion was shared by prominent American social scientists like Talcott Parsons, who argued that the "elements of continuity between Western agrarian populism and McCarthyism are not by any means purely fortuitous."

Gino Germani, an Italian-born sociologist who sought refuge from Mussolini's jails in Argentina only to later lose his academic job under Perón's government, set the research agenda for the study of Latin American populism and for the comparison between fascism and populism. Like Hofstadter, he viewed populism as a transitional stage provoked by the modernization of society. Relying on modernization and mass society theories, he argued that abrupt processes of modernization such as urbanization and industrialization produced masses in a state of anomie that became available for top-down mobilization. The social base of Peronism was the new working class, made up of recent migrants who were not socialized into working-class culture, and therefore a charismatic leader mobilized them. He wrote that populism had ambiguous effects on Argentinean democratization.

"The political incorporation of the popular masses started under totalitarianism. It gave workers an experience of political and social participation in their personal lives, annulling at the same time political organizations and the basic rights that are the pillars for any genuine democracy."

Hofstadter and Germani rightly showed the importance of analyzing populism as simultaneously inclusionary and autocratic. Populists challenged exclusions and politicized humiliations, resentments and fears. Yet they reduced the complexity of democratic politics to a struggle between two antagonistic camps. A populist leader, like Perón, was portrayed as the embodiment of the will of the homogeneous people, and even as their savior and redeemer, transforming politics into religious-like struggles. Yet for all their merits, these pioneer studies reduced class and interest-based politics to the alleged irrationality of the masses, especially of poor rural dwellers and recent migrants. Scholars showed that mass society theory wrongly viewed populist followers as irrational and populism as a transitional stage in the modernization of society. Michael Kazin in *The Populist Persuasion* wrote: "Since the late 50s historians and other scholars have persuasively demolished both the portrait of the initial Populists as irrational bigots and the idea that those who supported Populism were linked demographically to McCarthy's followers." Historian Charles Postel showed that U.S. populists were not backward-looking, but were modern and defended their interests in a movement that "resembled a type of reformist and evolutionary social democracy." Argentinean workers support for Perón was rational because as Secretary of Labor he addressed workers' demands for social security, higher wages, unionization and labor legislation.

Despite the empirical and theoretical inconsistencies of modernization theory, mass society and psychological theories, some European scholars adopted these approaches to explain the rise of right-wing populism in the 1980s and 90s. According to Hans-Georg Betz for example, "the emergence and rise of radical right-wing populist parties in the 1980s was a direct response to the transition from industrial welfare capitalism to postindustrial individualized capitalism." It reflected "to a large extent the psychological strain associated with uncertainties produced by large-scale socioeconomic and sociocultural changes." Their social base was made up of the losers from modernization. "The typical radical right-wing voter more often than not came from the lower classes, had only a low to moderate level of education, and tended to live in the disadvantaged areas of Western Europe's large and medium-sized cities." They directed their resentment to the political class, the administrative bureaucracy, immigrants and refugees.

When using mass society perspectives, scholars and journalists analyzed how rapid processes of social change produced masses in a state of anomie that fell prey to populist demagogues. The responses of populist followers are viewed as emotional and irrational. Thus, the theorist claims a moral and epistemic privileged position to distinguish the rational and desirable from the irrational and dangerous. What is modern is equated with the rational, meaning ideological or interest-based politics, while condemning populist politics as irrational and backward. As Robert B. Horwitz argues in *America's Right*, this approach labels "as irrational and reactionary those political actors and behaviors with which the researcher happens to disagree."

Emotional Appeal of Populism

It is not a surprise that many journalists and pundits use mass society theories to explain the rise and appeal of Trumpism as a revolt of rural non-educated voters who respond emotionally to his anti-globalization, xenophobic and anti-cosmopolitan appeals. It seemed to be comforting to blame the uneducated and the rural to wash down the shame of having white, educated middle-class men and women also voting for a misogynistic, xenophobic and racist candidate. But most importantly, the rigid distinction between the rational and the emotional does not work because populists, like other politicians, appeal to reasons and emotions, to economic interests and cultural values. If mass society theorists were right in showing the ambiguities of populism for democratization, they misrepresented their politics as irrational. The challenge is to understand the emotional and interest-based appeals of populism. As Chantal Mouffe wrote in her study of right-wing populism in Austria, rationalist frameworks prevent understanding "antagonism, as well as the role of passions, in the formation of collective identities."

Three approaches replaced mass society and historicist theories of populism that linked it to the early phases of modernization: discursive, political, and ideational theories.

Ernesto Laclau's Discourse Theory

Instead of focusing on the content of populist ideologies or on its class base, Ernesto Laclau developed a formal theory of populism and its logic of articulation. Populism is a political practice that creates popular political identities. In *Politics and Ideology in Marxist Theory*, he defined populism as a discourse that articulates popular democratic interpellations as antagonistic to the dominant ideology. Populist discourse polarizes the social field into two antagonistic and irreconcilable poles: the people vs. the power block. The types of populist ruptures, according to Laclau, are not theoretically predetermined, and could lead to fascism, socialism or to Perón's Bonapartism.

In his book *On Populist Reason*, Laclau contrasted everyday, mundane and administrative politics with those exceptional moments of a populist rupture, understood as the political. He argued that the division of society into two antagonistic camps was required to put an end to exclusionary institutional systems and to forge an alternative order. He contrasted the logic of difference and the logic of equivalence. The first presupposes that "any legitimate demand can be satisfied in a non-antagonistic, administrative way." There are demands that cannot be resolved individually and aggregate themselves, forming an equivalential chain. Under the logic of equivalence "all the demands in spite of their differential character, tend to aggregate themselves," becoming "fighting demands" that cannot be resolved by the institutional system. The social space splits into two camps: power and the underdog. The logic of populist articulation is anti-institutional; it is based on the construction of an enemy, and in a logic of equivalence that could lead to the rupture of the system. The name of the leader becomes the symbol that unites all the demands for change and renewal.

In *Posthegemony*, Jon Beasley-Murray wrote: "Laclau's project is a defense of populism." He failed, according to Beasley-Murray, because he relied on Carl Schmitt's view of politics as the struggle between friend and enemy. Under these constructs, it is difficult to imagine democratic adversaries who have legitimate institutional spaces. Enemies, as in Schmitt's view, might need to be manufactured and destroyed. Andrew Arato, in his groundbreaking critique of Laclau entitled "Political Theology and Populism," argued that populism might involve the extraction of the mythical people —as constructed and imagined by the leader or the theorist of populism— from the empirically existing population.

Enrique Peruzzotti writes in the *Routledge Handbook of Global Populism*, "Laclau turns the debate on populism upside down. Whereas populism appears as a normatively desirable outcome in politics, representative democracy is presented in terms of depoliticizing institutional machinery that seeks to neutralize the creative power of *the political.*" Laclau sustained that with the global rise of neoliberalism, understood as a rational and scientific mode of governance, public debate on the political economy was closed and replaced by the imposition of the criteria of experts. When all parties accepted neoliberalism and the rule of technocrats, citizens could not choose between alternatives. Politics was reduced to an administrative enterprise. Populism, Laclau argued, entails the renaissance of politics. It is a revolt against technocratic reasoning, the surrendering of national sovereignty to supranational institutions, and of the popular will to neoliberal political elites. Laclau's followers Iñigo Errejón (one of the ideologists of Podemos) and Chantal Mouffe maintain that the task of the left is to construct popular democratic subjects. Otherwise, right-wing populists will give expression to popular grievances by politicizing fears of immigration and multiculturalism.

Ernesto Laclau did not only favor populist ruptures in his scholarship; he was also an advisor to presidents Nestor and Cristina Kirchner in Argentina. He decried the lack of a populist rupture in his country of origin, where a stronger civil society and democratic institutions resisted attempts by the

Kirchners to follow the Chávez model of populist Bolivarian transformation. The leaders of the Spanish left-wing populist party Podemos used Laclau's theory and their experiences as advisors to the Bolivarian nations of Venezuela, Bolivia and Ecuador to successfully challenge Spain's two-party system.

Whereas Laclau and his followers are right in arguing that populism politicized neoliberal administrative orders, populist Schmittian views of the political are dangerous because they are anti-pluralist, and in the end antidemocratic. Populism attacks the institutions that are, in Richard Wolin's words in *The Frankfurt School Revisited*, "an indispensable bulwark against political despotism." Constitutionalism, the separation of powers, freedom of speech, assembly and the press are necessary for the politics of participatory democracy, to strengthen the public sphere and to allow independent social movements to push for their democratizing demands. Populists in power, even those that promise more democracy, target precisely the constitutional framework of democracy. Their systematic attacks on civil rights and liberties, and their attempts to control civil society and the public sphere, push democracies in crises toward authoritarianism.

A populist rupture takes place, according to Laclau, when there are crises of political representation because the institutional system cannot address demands individually. "This leads to an internal chasm within society and the construction of two antagonistic chains of equivalency." To understand how populist ruptures take place, I will briefly describe how Hugo Chávez in Venezuela, Evo Morales in Bolivia and Rafael Correa in Ecuador brought about populist ruptures. Then I will explore why ruptures did not take place in the Kirchner's Argentina and in Greece under Syriza.

Chávez, Morales and Correa got to power in contexts of profound crises of political representation and in all the institutions of democracy, such as congress and the judiciary. Parties were perceived as instruments of local and foreign elites that implemented neoliberal policies that increased social inequality. Parties collapsed as political outsiders rose to power with platforms that promised to wipe out corrupt politicians, to experiment with participatory forms of democracy, to strengthen the role of the state in the economy and to redistribute income and wealth.

The coalitions that brought leftist populists to power understood constituent power as a revolutionary force that ought to be permanently activated to refound, from scratch, all the corrupt political institutions of constituted power that served the interests of foreign powers and local elites. These leaders were elected with the promise to convene constitutional assemblies that, with the participation of social movements and common citizens, were tasked with the drafting of new constitutions. The new constitutions in Venezuela, Bolivia and Ecuador expanded citizens' rights while simultaneously concentrating power in the executive.

The second cause that explains these populist ruptures was widespread popular resistance to neoliberalism. On February 27, 1989, the Venezuelan Caracazo —a massive insurrection against the hike in the price of gasoline that was brutally repressed, with hundreds of citizens assassinated by the state— undermined and buried the legitimacy of Venezuela's two-party system. Between 1997 and 2005, the three elected presidents of Ecuador — Abdalá Bucaram (1996–97), Jamil Mahuad (1998–2000) and Lucio Gutiérrez (2003–2005)—were deposed by uprisings against neoliberalism and political corruption. From 2000 to 2003, Bolivia underwent a cycle of protest and political turmoil that resulted in the collapse of the party system established in 1985 and of the neoliberal economic model.

A third cause was that citizens perceived that politicians and neoliberal elites surrendered national sovereignty to the International Monetary Fund, the World Bank and to the U.S. government. Venezuela changed its pro third world oil and foreign policies and became an advocate of neoliberal reform and free trade. In a desperate move to stop hyperinflation in 2000, Ecuador gave up its national currency, the sucre, for the U.S. dollar. The government of Jamil Mahuad surrendered national sovereignty, allowing the U.S. to establish a military base to monitor illegal immigration and drug trafficking. Bolivia underwent social strife and widespread human rights abuses as the military unsuccessfully followed U.S. policies of forceful eradication of coca leaf production. These left-wing leaders proposed a counterproject to U.S.-dominated neoliberal trade initiatives. The Bolivarian Alliance for the Americas (ALBA) aimed for a real Latin American and Caribbean integration based on social justice and solidarity among the people. Their goals were to stop U.S. domination in the region by promoting Latin American unity and to create a multi-polar international system.

Nestor Kirchner came to power in 2003 in a conjuncture that could have led to a populist rupture. Political parties were in crisis, Argentina had just gone through a deep economic collapse in 2001-02, and there were strong movements of resistance to neoliberalism as workers took over factories and the unemployed occupied the streets and plundered supermarkets. Despite using a populist language of refoundation, the Kirchners were not committed to a populist rupture. But most importantly, their ambivalence in following the populist script was explained by how social movements and civil society reacted against what they perceived as authoritarian policies and practices. Thousands mobilized against Cristina Kirchner's agrarian policies. Her attempts to modify the constitution to allow for her reelection were resisted by civil society and an independent constitutional court. In sum, relatively stronger democratic institutions and a complex civil society were impediments to a populist rupture in Argentina.

As in Latin America, Syriza came to power after massive protests. In May 2011, the aganaktismenoi, a spontaneous grassroots movement, occupied squares to protest against the neoliberal policies of the Panhellenic Socialist Movement (PASOK) and the New Democracy (ND) center-right party. Giorgos Katsambekis writes in "Radical Left Populism in Contemporary Greece: Syriza's Trajectory from Minoritarian Opposition to Power," that Syriza won the 2015 election "staging a sharp antagonism between the vast majority of the people and a privileged minority that was profiting from the crisis." After obtaining 36% of the vote, Syriza was forced to enter into a coalition with a small right-wing populist and nationalist party, the Independent Greeks (ANEL). Contrary to the South American cases previously analyzed, neither the Greek parties nor the parliamentary system collapsed; nor did Syriza aim at overhauling democratic institutions via constitutional change. The regional context and pressures from the EU also played a key role at moderating the impulses of the new administration to not follow austerity policies. Syriza capitulated to the Troika in July 2015, even after winning a referendum against austerity policies. Its radical populist promises evaporated and the party became less democratic and more vertical and leader-centric. Journalist John Judis in *The Populist Explosion* claims that Syriza no longer "fights the establishment, but has in effect become the center-left component of it, as PASOK was."

Donald Trump captured the Republican Party in a context of a relative crisis of political parties, but not of a generalized collapse of all democratic institutions. He nonetheless ruptured the elite consensus that linked globalization with limited policies of multicultural recognition for women, non-whites and the LGBTQ communities. Whereas it will be easier to get rid of multiculturalism and "political correctness" to please misogynist, homophobic, nationalist, racist and xenophobic constituencies, it would be more difficult to abandon globalization, especially by an administration committed to the unregulated market and to dismantling the regulatory welfare state.

His election nonetheless ruptured America's neoliberal multicultural consensus embraced by Republican and Democratic Party elites, which linked globalization with the limited recognition of minorities' cultural rights. As a candidate, he opposed NAFTA and the Trans-Pacific Partnership agreement. In power, he entered into trade wars with China. He linked national decline with the absence of industrial production. He promised to bring manufacturing jobs back to the U.S. and thus erected tariffs, breaking with the Republican faith in free global trade. President Trump might be able to at least symbolically slow down manufacturing outsourcing, and might be able to keep some manufacturing jobs in the U.S. Yet his nationalist protectionist policies will not stop automation and other structural sources of industrial job depletion.

Trump used blatant racist tropes against Muslims and Mexicans, destroying the myth that the U.S. was becoming a colorblind, post-racial society. Elites and many citizens believed that the election of their first African-American president showed that the U.S. was moving to a colorblind post racial order, that overt racism was a thing of the past, and that the goals of the civil rights movement were achieved. When launching his presidential candidacy from Trump Tower in New York City he asserted, "When Mexico sends its people, they're not sending their best... They're bringing drugs. They're bringing crime. They're rapists. And some I assume, are good people." He expanded his xenophobic and racist platform by calling Muslims terrorists and promising to monitor Muslims within the U.S. and banning those who want to enter the country.

Trump was the heir to the Tea Party, a right-wing insurrection against the first non-white president and to his limited policies of redistribution, such as universal health care. Donald Trump, a Birther who denied Obama's Americanness, reached beyond the Tea Party social base of white, older, wealthier and more educated conservatives, appealing also to the white working-class. His base of support was not only made up of the losers of globalization and uneducated white males. Middle-class, educated white men and women also supported him because many felt that they were not getting their fair share, and that they faced economic insecurity in their lives. They felt that women, blacks, Hispanics and gays were empowered by unfair policies of affirmative action and political correctness that negatively targeted white heterosexual males. Sociologist Arlie Hochschild in *Strangers in their Own Land* explains that Trump's followers "also felt culturally marginalized: their views about abortion, gay marriage, gender roles, race, guns, and the Confederate flag all were held in ridicule in the national media as backward. And they felt part of a demographic decline... They'd begun to feel like a besieged minority." It remains to be seen the extent to which Trump's administration will dismantle the institutions and policies of the last decades that linked open markets and globalization to the limited cultural inclusion of minorities, women and the LGBTQ communities.

Following Laclau, populism emerges when there are widespread crises of political representation. When all democratic institutions are in crises, populists are able to rupture the neoliberal order, draft new constitutions, create new political institutions and change their foreign policies. When populists got to power in conditions of a relative crisis of political representation, as in Greece or Argentina, stronger domestic and supranational institutions contained populist challenges. Populist ruptures also took place in presidentialist systems, whereas parliamentary systems often forced populists to enter into pacts and agreements, de-radicalizing their platforms. Trump may rupture policies of multicultural recognition, but might not be willing or able to stop economic globalization.

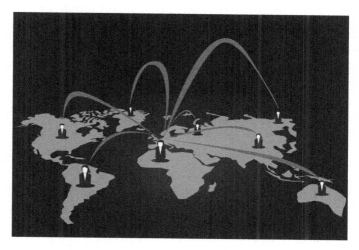

2. Image that symbolizes the networks of globalization. Some authors attribute the rise in populisms to the uncertainty and loss that structural changes brought on by globalization have created in certain sectors of the population.

Political Theories

Kurt Weyland argued that the domain of populism is politics because it is "a specific way of competing for and exercising political power." Political theorists study populism as a political style or as a political strategy. Benjamin Moffitt defined populism as a style "that features an appeal to the people vs. the elite," which uses what elites consider bad manners such as accent, body language, bad taste, and the performance of what are perceived as crises, breakdowns or threats. These performances are related to distrust in the complexities of modern governance. Populists offer swift action rather than negotiation and deliberation. The author of *The Global Rise of Populism* focuses on what is "performed and done, rather than just a set of ideas or ways of organizing followers."

Definitions of populism as a political style focus on the mobilizing, performative and expressive aspects of populism. According to Weyland, "defining populism as political style therefore casts too wide a net and hinders the clear delimitation of cases." With the goal of providing a minimum definition that would eliminate conceptual disagreement and advance the accumulation of knowledge, Weyland in his groundbreaking article "Clarifying a Contested Concept: Populism in the Study of Latin American Politics," defined populism "as a political strategy through which a personalistic leader seeks or exercises government power based on direct, unmediated, uninstitutionalized support from large numbers of mostly unorganized followers." Rather than hewing to any particular political ideology, or to right and left distinctions, populist leaders are pragmatic and opportunistic in their quest to conquer and retain power.

Political theories of populism have correctly emphasized the importance of political leaders, many of them charismatic. These theories were useful to develop typologies of Latin American populism, and to explore how it was adapted to different developmental strategies: nationalist and state-led import substitution (that sought to produce locally the manufacturing products that were imported) in the 1940s, neoliberalism in the 1990s, and the return of state-led development and nationalism in the first decades of the twenty-first century.

Studies of populism as a political strategy showed that leaders and followers were not always linked by formal institutions, but tended to exaggerate the supposedly unmediated relationship between leaders and followers. As will be shown in Chapter 3, populist parties in Latin America, for example, were organized through formal bureaucratic party networks and clientelist informal networks that distributed resources, information and jobs to the poor. Like other political parties, populists exchanged services for votes. But in addition, populist exchanges went together with a discourse that portrayed common people as the essence of the nation, creating political and cultural identities.

Political theorists agree with Laclau in arguing that populism is a specific type of response to the crises of political representation. According to Kenneth Roberts, it is a "political strategy for appealing to mass constituencies where representative institutions are weak or discredited, and where various forms of social exclusion or political marginalization leave citizens alienated from such institutions." It first emerged when excluded people without partisan loyalty where enfranchised for the first time. Examples of this first populist incorporation are the first wave of populism in Latin America in the 1930s to the 1970s, Thaksin Shinawatra in Thailand, and the populist movements that emerged in Africa after democratization in the 1990s.

A second crisis of political representation was produced by political systems, such as Venezuela's two-party system, when they became unresponsive and unaccountable in the 1990s. Hugo Chávez rebelled against closed, self-interested and self-reproducing cartel parties. The Populist Party emerged in the U.S. when in the 1890s, according to Charles Postel in *The Populist Vision*, "two firmly entrenched parties dominated the political scene. At the national level, Democrats and Republicans held much in common as they shared a conservatism that was acceptable to the financial and corporate establishment." Similarly, Podemos and Syriza revolted against party systems where the right and social democrats followed the same Troika-inspired neoliberal policies that led to the de-politicization of citizens and their transformation into consumers. The National Rally (formerly National Front), as Mabel Berezin shows in *Illiberal Politics in Neoliberal Times*, opposed the party consensus of integration into the European Union, politicizing the loss of national sovereignty, anti-globalization and anti-immigration feelings.

A third scenario for a crisis of political representation, according to Kenneth Roberts, occurs when "political representation and political competition tend to become highly personalized, voters support and identify with leaders rather than party organizations or platforms, and the axis of political competition are likewise drawn between rival personalities who claim to better represent the true interests of the people." Under these conditions a series of populist leaders, political outsiders and personalist leaders emerged and rose to power in Ecuador and Peru.

In nations such as Costa Rica, Uruguay and Western liberal democracies with strong party systems and functioning liberal democracies upholding the rule of law, populism was confined to the margins. When European right-wing or left-wing populists got to power, they were in coalition with other parties and had to de-radicalize their demands. Moreover, as Rovira Kaltwasser and Taggart show in their edited issue of the journal *Democratization* on populism in power, strong domestic political institutions and supranational organizations within the European Union for the most part, and with the exceptions of Hungary and Poland, restrained the undemocratic impulses of right-wing populist parties.

Weyland, in his chapter in *The Oxford Handbook of Populism*, argues for the need to distinguish populist from fascist. Whereas the later abolished democracy, populism thrives in the hybrid zone between democracy and competitive authoritarianism. He also differentiates ideological right-wing parties from non-ideological, opportunistic and purely pragmatic populist parties. Whereas a strong ideology cements the loyalty of a reduced cadre, populist parties like the National Rally under Marine Le Pen, Podemos, Syriza and Viktor Orbán's Fidesz are flexible and pragmatic in their ideological appeals. For example, in the 2016 elections Podemos claimed that they and not the PSOE were the real social democratic party. After winning a referendum against austerity, Syriza accepted the neoliberal package of the Troika. Marine Le Pen transformed the National Front not only by expelling her father, but by abandoning anti-Semitism and homophobia to portray herself as the defender of Western civilization against Islam.

Political theories of populism use normative liberal notions of democracy, and therefore can show the conditions under which populism could lead to inclusion or to authoritarianism. When populism first emerged, it included previously excluded citizens in the political community. Under Juan Domingo Perón's first two terms in office, for example, voter turnout dramatically surged from 18% of the population in 1946 to 50% in 1955. His administration expanded the franchise by giving women the right to vote in 1951. Perón's government redistributed wealth and increased the share of wages in the national Gross Domestic Product from 37% in 1946 to 47% in 1955. Populist inclusion under Perón did not foster or strengthen democracy. As with other populists, he concentrated power in the hands of the presidency, attacked the media, aimed to control civil society and provoked radical sectors of the opposition to topple him with a coup d'état. Hence, inclusion did not lead to the creation of democratic political cultures or institutions that could process conflicts. Populism was experienced as a struggle between two antagonistic camps.

In democratizing settings like Thailand, populism contributed to processes of political inclusion at the cost of democratic institutionalization, just as it did in Latin America from the 1930s to the 1970s. Thaksin Shinawatra benefited from the 1997 constitution that strengthened the role of elected officials over the military and the monarchy. He was the first democratically elected prime minister to complete a full term in office. A billionaire who made a fortune in mobile phone technology, he was a technocrat for most of his tenure from 2001 to 2006. Yet in 2004 when his popularity was wavering he started to appeal to the people, gave handouts to poor voters in rural areas and the urban informal sector, and transformed his persona to be a man of the people.

Like his Latin American counterparts, Thaksin Shinawatra included the poor materially by creating health programs, giving debt relief to rural cultivators and introducing a loan system for low-income university students. Under Thaksin, poverty fell from 21.3% to 11.3%. He led the political involvement of the informal sector, the rural poor, urban middle classes and the northern small business and landowners. Yet simultaneusly he disdained opponents, used dismissive remarks about Muslims in the South, promoted extrajudicial killings of drug addicts, attacked the independent media, bullied nongovernmental organizations, and his politics of polarization and closure of democratic spaces for the opposition led to coups against him in 2006, and against his sister Yingluck in 2014. Like other populists, he led to the polarization of his nation and the deinstitutionalization of democracy that ended in military interventions.

Populists, Weyland argues, undermine democracy in two ways. The first is that their closure of democratic spaces to the opposition leads the more radical and undemocratic opponent to plot military coups. The first wave of populism in Latin America was characterized by the cycle of populist government-coup d'état. Yet military interventions are costly and risky, because the international community nowadays only accepts elections as the legitimate means of regime change. Currently, and with few exceptions, populism does not end with a coup; rather, Weyland argues, populists undermine democracy from within. Steven Levitsky and James Loxton in "Populism and Competitive Authoritarianism in the Andes" show how populists pushed weak presidentialist democracies in Latin America into competitive authoritarianism for three reasons: (1)

Populists were outsiders with no experience in the give and take of parliamentary politics; (2) they were elected with the mandate to refound existing political institutions, meaning the institutional framework of liberal democracy; and (3) they confronted congress, the judiciary and other institutions controlled by parties. In order to win elections, populists skewed the electoral playing field. As incumbents they had extraordinary advantages, such as using state media, selectively silencing the privately-owned media, harassing the opposition, controlling electoral tribunal boards and all instances of appeal, and using public funds to influence the election. When these presidents won elections, the voting moments were clean, but the electoral processes blatantly favored incumbents. Populists like Hugo Chávez, Rafael Correa or Alberto Fujimori displaced democracies toward competitive authoritarianism.

If the strength of political theories is to explain the process of democratic erosion, their institutionalist views of democracy are not always the best to take into account populist critiques of real existing democracies. Populists promise to correct the deficits of participation and representation of liberal democracies. Populists challenge the appropriation of political sovereignty by political and economic elites, the reduction of politics to an administrative enterprise and the depoliticization of democracy. Populists invoke the transformative power of constituent power over constituted power. Liberals are rightly afraid of the dangers of appeals to the unbounded power of the sovereign people to create new constitutions and institutions. Yet some tend to idealize the institutions of constituted power. The powerful populist critique of the malfunctions and deficits of democracy needs to be addressed without idealizing the existing institutional systems of real existing liberal democracies.

By focusing exclusively on institutions, political theorists do not pay enough attention to the public sphere and other forums where citizens form and voice their political opinions. Populists do not only challenge the institutional framework of democracy, they can also threaten the democratic processes of forming political opinions when they enter into a war against the media or when they impose their views as the only acceptable truth. Trump, for instance, might not destroy the institutional framework of democracy, but he has damaged the inclusive and tolerant public sphere. Hate speech, the disregard for journalistic practices to find the facts, and blind loyalty to his words as the only truthful ones has disfigured the foundations of democratic public spheres in the U.S.

Populism as a Set of Ideas

Ideational approaches, like political theories, aim to construct minimal definitions that can be used for empirical comparative analysis. Instead of focusing on the strategies or style of leaders, or on their charisma, they study populism as a set of ideas on how the world is and should be. Kirk Hawkins wrote, "populism is a set of fundamental beliefs about the nature of the political world." Cas Mudde defined populism as:

"an ideology that considers society to be ultimately separated into two homogeneous and antagonistic groups, 'the pure people' versus 'the corrupt elite,' and which argues that politics should be an expression of the volonté générale (general will) of the people."

Lacking the sophistication of other ideologies, such as socialism or liberalism, it is a thin-centered ideology and is combined with other beliefs and ideas of politics. Therefore, it could be associated with nativism and neoliberalism in Austria, or with anti-neoliberal and anti-racist platforms in Greece with Syriza and Podemos in Spain. The role of the leader is not central to this approach, because it focuses on the ideologies of movements, parties, and even attitudes of a population.

Mudde and Rovira Kaltwasser use the ideational approach to distinguish between inclusionary and exclusionary forms of populism. The former, which they consider mostly applies to Latin American variants, aims to include the materially, politically and symbolically excluded, while right-wing variants in Australia, Europe and the U.S. seek the exclusion of Muslims, immigrants and non-white populations.

Even though their focus on geographical differences did not work, as Syriza and Podemos do not use xenophobia and are more similar to Latin American than right-wing European variants, their pioneering work set an agenda to differentiate variants of populism.

Sociologist Dani Filc in his article "Latin American Inclusive and European Exclusionary Populism: Colonialism as an Explanation" argues that distinct legacies of colonialism partially explain different uses of ethnicity to construct the people. "Colonialism established two differentiated worlds, the metropolitan polity for which ideas such as the sovereign people, democratic citizenship and rights were relevant," and their external peripheries made up of savages, the natives and the Orientals. Former colonial powers in Europe or imperialist nations with a white national identity like the U.S. used notions of white superiority to stigmatize non-white immigrants, many of them arriving from their former colonies as racially inferior and as bearers of cultures that are antagonistic to the West. Exclusionary populists use nativism and xenophobia to appeal to a common past in which immigrants and non-whites do not belong. Inclusionary ethnic appeals work in postcolonial contexts where the natives or the indigenous, who are also the poor, are the victims of discrimination as well as of exclusion. In Bolivia and other postcolonial nations, the excluded are the core of the people and the nation, while in Filc's words "the oligarchy, imperialism, and colonialism are the absolute Other." Yet exclusionary constructs of ethnicity were also used in India and Brazil. Narendra Modi rose through the ranks of Hindu nationalist organizations with an anti-Muslim and antiestablishment agenda. He benefited from politicizing anti-Muslim feelings and nationalist issues that aim to restore "India's old grandeur." Jair Bolsonaro used racist and misogynist tropes to argue for law and order, depicting the military regimes of the 1960s and 1970s as a time of economic prosperity without insecurity.

3. Sculptural image of Human Rights. Paris, France.

Ideational theories have several methodological and theoretical problems. Kirk Hawkins in *Venezuela's Chavismo and Populism in Comparative Perspective* innovatively adapted holistic grading from pedagogy to measure populist discourse. He distinguished pluralist from populist speeches. Yet his understanding of discourse is limited to words and does not encompass performances, actions, and social and historical contexts. His sophisticated statistical analysis yielded some false positives, like considering George W. Bush a populist when he clearly was not. Ideational definitions use the term ideology as a catchall concept. Contrary to other ideologies, populists do not have foundational texts, and it is difficult to conceptualize a distinct populist ideology. By subsuming all cases where a "populist ideology" was used as a case for populism, they overextend the term to encompass the ideologies of political parties, social movements and citizen's perception. The Indignados movement in Spain used a populist rhetoric to demand "real democracy," but it was a leaderless horizontal movement. Only when a group of political science professors created the party, Podemos, under strong leadership from Pablo Iglesias, a leadership that has been questioned by some of its militants because of its verticalist and not fully-democratic nature, did Podemos become populist.

Ideational theorists also consider populism as the attitudes of a population. For example, Mudde and Rovira Kaltwasser in *Populism: A Very Short Introduction* wrote: "there is a dormant Hugo Chávez or Sarah Palin inside all of us. The question is how does she or he become activated?" This assertion is problematic, because every idea that appeals to the people against the elite invoking the general will is branded as populism. So, for instance, when many Chileans want to change

Pinochet's constitution it could appear they are endorsing populist ideas, when perhaps they are not. Most troublesome, by claiming that there is a Trump inside all of us, they are normalizing populist autocrats because, after all, they awakened the dormant tyrant inside all of us. Who are the "us" that Mudde and Rovira Kaltwasser write about? African Americans, feminists, LGBTQ activists and white progressives in general do not have a dormant Sarah Palin inside all of them; on the contrary, they are resisting Trump's attacks on democracy.

In their effort to not make normative assumptions about the relationship between populism and democracy, Mudde and Rovira Kaltwasser rely on empiricist arguments that see populism as both a corrective and a threat to democracy. However, it is a stretch of the imagination to see the likes of Geert Wilders, Jean Marie or Marine Le Pen and Donald Trump as correctives to democracy. They even defend right-wing European populism, arguing that the problem of populist exclusion is nativism and has nothing to do with populism. Mudde and Rovira Kaltwasser's lack of a normative theory of democracy does not allow them to criticize the internal logic of populism. Even though they show the institutional and contextual conditions under which populism can lead to de-democratization or democratization, they do not have an explicit normative theory to criticize autocratic populists.

Instead, they sneak in their preference for liberal democracy without making their normative theory explicit. The populist view of politics as struggles between antagonistic enemies, while effective in rupturing existing institutional arrangements, often leads to anti-pluralist practices and policies that under conditions of weak institutions and fragile civil societies can lead to the slow death of democracy and its replacement with authoritarianism.

Finally, the root of populism, as Nadia Urbinati argues in *The Routledge Handbook of Global Populism*, is not associated with giving back power to the people as a whole or to Rousseau's general will, but rather to one of its parts: the masses that are outside the establishment. As Arato and Cohen wrote in "Civil Society, Populism and Religion," populism entails a *pars pro toto* logic that constructs a part of the population as the authentic people who stand for the sovereign whole.

What is Populism?

Building on dialogues with the approaches discussed above, and with critical theorists Nadia Urbinati, Jean L. Cohen, Federico Finchelstein, Enrique Peruzzotti, Andrew Arato, Silvio Waisbord, Felipe Burbano, Benjamín Arditi and others, I understand populism as political discourses and strategies that aim to rupture institutional systems by polarizing society into two antagonistic camps. I differentiate social movements that use a populist rhetoric of the people against the establishment from populism. Without the presence of a leader, as Nadia Urbinati wrote in *Democracy Disfigured*, "a popular movement that uses a populist rhetoric (i.e., polarization and anti-representative discourse) is not yet populism." Populist leaders claim that they represent and even embody the interests, will and aspirations of a homogeneous people. All of those who challenge their claim to be the incarnation of the people are branded as enemies of the people, the leader and the nation. Populists do not face political adversaries; they confront enemies at the symbolic level. As Perón put it, when political adversaries become "enemies of the nation" they are no longer "gentlemen that one should fight fairly but snakes that one can kill in any way."

Populist parties seeking power need to be distinguished from populists in power. Whereas populists challenge the system or the establishment by promising to give power to the people, once in power they show their true anti-pluralist and antidemocratic colors. Once in office, populists concentrate power in the hands of the executive, disregard the division of power and the rule of law, and attack dissident voices in the public sphere and civil society. When populists assume power in conditions of crises of political representation and with weak democratic institutions, they displace democracy toward authoritarianism.

In more institutionalized political systems, they disfigure democracy by reducing its complexity to a Manichaean struggle between the leader as the embodiment of the people and its enemies.

Right-wing and left-wing variants of populism are not the same. To a large extent, the difference lies in how they imagine and construct the people. This category can be conceived with religious, ethnic or political criteria, and as a diverse population or as a homogeneous actor. Constructs of the people as a community of believers, even when these communities are imagined as egalitarian, inherently exclude nonbelievers. Vedi R. Hadiz in his volume *Islamic Populism* shows how the *ummah* of Islamic populism is made up of internally diverse social interests, homogenized as those pious members of the community who possess virtue through juxtaposition against immoral elites and their foreign non-Islamic allies. Similarly, the three Israeli populist parties, the ultra-orthodox Mizrahi party "Shas," Israel Our Home and the Likud party, are inclusionary to the community of believers while excluding nonbelievers. Likewise in Western Europe and the U.S., Christianity, Judeo Christianity or Christian-Secularism is politicized as an identity against Islam. Some European populist parties proclaim to be defenders of Western civilization, secularism and individual freedoms by casting Islam as the antithetical and inassimilable ultimate Other. Olivier Roy wrote in *Saving the People* that religion in Europe and the U.S. is a marker of cultural identity that enables them to distinguish the good us from the bad them, understood in essentialist and ahistorical terms. "Christian identity for populists is strongly linked to a romanticized idea about how things were." It promotes mobilizations to reconquer the public space as Christian, and even the human body by opposing circumcision and halal food.

Some populist movements in Europe and the U.S., as well as Jair Bolsonaro in Brazil and Narendra Modi in India, use ethnicity to exclude minority populations. The people as constructed by Donald Trump, for example, confronts ethnic and cultural enemies such as Muslims, Mexicans or militant black activists. The image of the Mexican, as most Latinos in the U.S. are nowadays called, is built on longstanding nationalist stereotypes that marked them as lazy, dangerous and as the ultimate outsiders to the U.S. nation. Regardless of whether Mexicans and other Latino populations have lived for long periods in the U.S., they are regarded as recent and passing immigrants, and as freeloaders who drain white taxpayers. The notion of the Muslim terrorist is not only a xenophobic reaction to 9/11. It is also built on the legacies of the image of the U.S. as a Christian nation. Contrary to Latinos and Muslims, who can be attacked with blatantly racist words, Trump as well as the Tea Party and other conservatives use code words of law and order to mark the unruly black militant as a criminal and as the opposite of the law-abiding and taxpaying citizen.

The Tea Party and Trumpism, for example, contrast a virtuous white, hardworking, taxpaying and law-abiding middle class against black and other dependents of color who are below, and the controlling liberal and cosmopolitan elites above. Similarly, right-wing European populists defend the ordinary people against those below such as immigrants, refugees and former colonial subjects, and the privileged New Class above.

Contrary to the exclusionary and racist view of the people as white, Evo Morales and his political party the MAS, as Raúl L. Madrid in *The Rise of Ethnic Politics in Latin America* shows, successfully used inclusive ethnopopulist appeals. Given the fluidity of race and ethnic relations in Bolivia, they were able to create an inclusionary ethnic party grounded in indigenous social movements that appealed to different indigenous groups while also incorporating mestizo organizations and candidates.

An alternative conceptualization of the people is primarily political and socioeconomic. Left-wing populists in Latin America and Southern Europe construct the category of the people as the majorities in their nations who are excluded by neoliberal policies imposed by supranational organizations like the IMF or the Troika. Podemos, for example, used an antagonistic discourse that aimed to rupture Spain's institutional system. They constructed an enemy, branded as "the caste," which has dominated political, economic, social and cultural life since the pacted transition to democracy in the mid-1970s. "The caste" is in an antagonistic relationship with the people, understood as the disenfranchised victims of neoliberalism. Similarly, Alexis Tsipras, the leader of Syriza, constructed the antagonism between the people and the neoliberal establishment in political and socioeconomic terms. Mélenchon also refuses left and right distinctions, claiming that when he gets to power his party will not follow class-based politics, but politics for the people.

Hugo Chávez framed the political arena so that he did not face political rivals, but instead an oligarchy that he defined as the political enemy of the people, "those self-serving elites who work against the homeland." His rhetoric politicized relationships of inequality between different classes and ethnic groups. He reclaimed Venezuela's indigenous and black heritages that were downplayed by the elites. According to Sujatha Fernandes in her volume *Who Can Stop the Drums*, Chávez tapped into the "deep reservoir of daily humiliation and anger felt by people of the lower classes."

As Jürgen Habermas pointed out, "'the people' does not comprise a subject with a will and consciousness. It only appears in the plural, and as a people, it is capable of neither decision nor action as a whole." Following these constructs, democrats imagine the people as a plurality of actors with different views and proposals. By constructing the people as plural, democrats face democratic rivals that have legitimate institutional and normative spaces.

On the contrary, populists like Donald Trump or Hugo Chávez claim, according to Jan Werner Müller in *What is Populism?*, "that they and only they represent the true people." Donald Trump, for example, has a unitary view of the people. In a rally in Florida he said, "The only important thing is the unification of the people – because the other people don't mean anything."

Chávez constructed the "people" as a sacred entity with a single consciousness and a will that could be embodied in his persona, built as the redeemer of the people. Chávez boasted, "This is not about Hugo Chávez; this is about a 'people.' I represent, plainly, the voice and the heart of millions." On another occasion he commanded, "I demand absolute loyalty to me. I am not an individual, I am the people." Even though Chávez's populist political and socioeconomic construction of the people was inclusionary, his view of the people-as-one was anti-pluralist, and in the end antidemocratic because he attempted to become its only voice.

Contrary to autocratic constructs of the people as one, left-wing populist parties like Syriza, Podemos and Morales's MAS have plural views of the people. Yet at times these leaders attempt to be the only voice of the people. When indigenous people from the lowlands challenged Morales's policies on mineral extraction, they were dismissed as having been manipulated by foreign NGOs and not as authentically indigenous. Morales's regime attempted to construct an indigenous identity centered on loyalty to his government, and which excluded and delegitimized all those who opposed him. But because of the power of social movements in whose name he argues he is ruling, Morales has not been allowed to impose his vision of the people-as-one. In contemporary Bolivia, according to anthropologist Nancy Postero, there is an "ongoing struggle to define who counts as *el pueblo boliviano*, and what that means for Bolivian democracy." Similar tensions between the populist leaders attempting to be the only voice of the people and the resistance of their constituencies to become embodied in the voice of the leader occurs in Syriza and Podemos. Their constituencies have not succumbed to their leaders' claim to be the only voice of the people.

	People as One	People as Plural
Religious politicization of fear-survival-exclusion	Israel: Shas, Israel Our Home, Likud. Turkey: Recep Tayyip Erdogan.	
Cultural-Ethnic-politicization of fear-survival	American and European Right-wing Populists. India: Narendra Modi. Brazil: Jair Bolsonaro	Bolivia: Ethno-populism of Evo Morales.
Political/ socioeconomic politicization of humiliations, injustice, resentment	Venezuela: Hugo Chávez. Ecuador: Rafael Correa.	Southern Europe's Left-wing Populism: Podemos, Syriza, La France Insoumise.

Table 1. Constructing the people

As Table 1 illustrates, when ethnic or religious views of the people are combined with constructs of the people as one, populism becomes exclusionary and antidemocratic. Under these conditions, populism can be a threat to the basic values of modernity such as a plural, critical and inclusive civil society. Political and socioeconomic constructions of the people can lead to inclusionary policies. Yet when "the people" is viewed as one, as Chávez did, his populism was inclusionary and antidemocratic because he assumed that the part of the people he embodied was the only authentic people. Pluralist views of the socioeconomic and political people can be inclusionary and lead to more democracy. Yet as the cases of Morales and Tsipras illustrate, these leaders tried to be the only voice of the people.

Chapter 2

Populist Leadership

This chapter differentiates horizontal leaderless movements from populism that is centered on a strong leader. Michael Hardt and Antonio Negri wrote in *Assembly*, "populism is thus characterized by a central paradox: constant lip service to the power of the people but ultimately control and decision-making by a small clique of politicians." Contrary to horizontal movements of the multitude that speak through many voices, under populism the people and the nation speak with one voice, that of a small clique of politicians and ultimately the voice of the leader. The rebellions of 2011 like the Arab Spring, the Indignados or Occupy Wall Street are better characterized as horizontal and leaderless insurgencies. As Benjamín Arditi explains in his chapters in *The Promise and Perils of Populism*, these protests were unplanned, sporadic and ethereal. They downplayed the role of the leader, celebrated general assemblies, used the web and occupations. "Insurgencies are more about opening up possibilities than designing a new order." Yet insurgencies were learning experiences, and led to cognitive shifts. Some informal leaders of these insurrections later became activists of populist parties.

The U.S. Peoples Party known as the Populist Party, an alliance or confederation of farmers, workers unions, temperance associations, women's groups and other reformist movements, was a powerful protest movement that lacking a strong leader remained at the margins of the political system. Laura Grattan's *Populism's Power* shows the democratic innovations of the Populists, such as grassroots political education, farmers' cooperatives and active participation in strikes. She maintains that crucial to the coalitional character of the People's Party was their ability to call the people together, "but also to find rhetoric that could leave 'the people' open ended." The horizontal nature of the movement did not translate well into the electoral policies of a third party. Their candidate, James Weaver, won 8.5% of the vote in 1892, wining majorities in Colorado, Idaho and Nevada, and pluralities in Kansas and North Dakota. In 1894 the Populist Party did better, conquering seven seats in the House and six in the Senate. Yet after its failed alliance with the Democratic Party in 1896 under William Jennings Bryan's candidacy, the Populist Party, which had split over its decision of supporting Bryan, ultimately disintegrated.

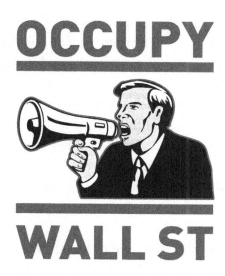

4. Occupy Wall Street was a popular insurgency without clear leadership, inspired by the 15M movement in Spain. Its objective was to continually occupy Wall Street, the financial district in New York, as a protest against the insecurity created by the global economic crisis.

Paolo Gerbaudo uses the term "populism of the leaderless people" to describe horizontal and leaderless movements like the anti-austerity Indignados in Spain and Greece, Occupy Wall Street, the Arab Spring in Tunisia and Egypt, Gezi Park protests in Turkey, the Movimento de Junho in Brazil in 2011 and France's Nuit Debout in 2016. He shows the importance of occupying public spaces and their transformation into agoras of democratic innovation. The author of *The Mask and The Flag* rightly shows, for example, the differences between the leaderless 15-M "citizenism movement" in Spain and the pivotal role of the charismatic and personalized leadership of Pablo Iglesias, the secretary general of Podemos. Yet Gerbaudo uses the term populism indistinguishably to brand horizontal movements and vertical parties. The Indignados that used a populist rhetoric and demanded to establish a real participatory democracy without intermediations were a leaderless horizontal movement of protest that avoided entering into the political system. In contrast, Podemos under the leadership of Iglesias is populist. In an article published in 2015 in the *New Left Review*, Pablo Iglesias wrote that Spaniards did not feel represented by the left-right categories, "our objective of identifying a new 'we'… initially came together around the signifier 'Pablo Iglesias.'" Similarly, as Nadia Urbinati sustains, until Trump came along the Tea Party was a movement in search of a leader. Under Trump's leadership, the movement simultaneously extended its appeal to new constituencies and became subordinated to a charismatic populist leader.

The concept of charisma has been used to analyze populism since Gino Germani wrote his seminal essays on Peronism in the 1950s. In *Reinventing the Italian Right*, Carlo Ruzza and Stefano Fella use the concept of charisma to analyze Silvio Berlusconi and

Umberto Bossi's leadership. Pedro Zúquete uses the category Missionary Politics to analyze Jean Marie Le Pen, Umberto Bossi and Hugo Chávez. Danielle Resnick uses charisma to discuss the populist strategies of Jacob Zuma in South Africa and Michael Sata in Zambia. Michael Sata viewed himself as the people's liberator, proclaiming: "Zambia needs a redeemer, Zambians want Moses to redeem them, and I am the redeemer of Zambia!" Populist leaders emerged in moments of distress that realigned socioeconomic and political relations. Followers transformed charismatic leaders into moral archetypes, exemplary figures that ought to be followed. Charismatic leaders are assimilated with religious, nationalist and other myths. Yet with few exceptions, such as Pedro Zúquete's work on Missionary Politics and Marco Garrido's "Why the Poor Support Populism," the affinities between charisma and populism are rarely theorized. In this chapter I use Weber to discuss populist charismatic leadership.

The Redemptive Mission of the Leader

In *Economy and Society* Max Weber wrote, "the bearer of charisma enjoys loyalty and authority by virtue of a mission believed to be embodied in him." Leaders become moral archetypes, exemplary figures that ought to be followed. According to Weber, leaders have to prove their charisma "in the eyes of their adherents." Having performed a heroic act often proves their charisma. Chávez led an unsuccessful coup attempt in 1992 against president Carlos Andrés Pérez. After failing, he said two very important phrases that were remembered by Venezuelans: "I assume the responsibility" and "for now." In their biography of Hugo Chávez, journalists Cristina Marcano and Alberto Barrera Tyszka explained the novelty of his words. "The former were a rarity in a country where politicians never seemed able to assume responsibility for anything." The latter sounded like a threat or "a cliff-hanger to a cinematic thriller." Chávez, the officer who led a failed coup, became the symbol of the democratic fight against a corrupt neoliberal political establishment. His military red beret became an icon of defiance against a failed and closed democracy, and many Venezuelans started to proudly wear it.

In the absence of a heroic performance, leaders and their close circle of followers try to mythologize their achievements and life stories. Zúquete writes that Jean Marie Le Pen's inner circle worked as apostles to sanctify the image of their leader. In the eyes of the militants of the National Front, Jean Marie Le Pen "appears as a true authentic leader. His life story, his role as the founder of the party, and all the perceived campaign of hatred against him dramatically bolster his leadership credentials... He offers a powerful example to follow and to emulate." Similarly, Rafael Correa claimed that he was extraordinary because he studied with scholarships, and that he dedicated his life to serve others. He was a leader of the catholic university student movement, a lay missionary with indigenous people and a world recognized scholar. His story, however, proved to be an exaggeration. Journalist Mónica Almeida and Ana Karina López in their biography of Correa entitled *El Séptimo Rafael* showed that he only had a one-year scholarship while attending high school; he did not earn merit scholarships to study in Louvain or at the University of Illinois at Urbana, and did not excel as a scholar.

Populist leaders, even when they don't, claim to come from humble and working-class origins. Due to their hard work, superior intelligence and self-interest in serving their nations and their peoples, they acquire their extraordinariness. These claims can be comical, as when Donald Trump said that he started his business empire with a one million dollar loan. Jean Marie Le Pen claimed to come from underprivileged beginnings, and that his ancestors were fishermen and peasants. Correa claimed to come from a working-class background, when he was actually the child of a downwardly mobile middle-class family with ties to the elite.

In my volume *Populist Seduction in Latin America*, I show how populist Ecuadorean Abdalá Bucaram presented himself as a person from a humble background who not only understood the people but also belonged to *el pueblo*. Because he was the son of Lebanese immigrants, he was discriminated against by the elites who considered him a parvenu with poor taste and bad habits. Bucaram's claim to be part of *el pueblo* was also illustrated by his way of speaking; his penchant for guayaberas and jeans; his passion for playing soccer; his way of eating with a spoon like the poor, rather than a fork and a knife like the rich; and by his love for popular Ecuadorian cooking. Like other populist leaders, Abdalá sought to make clear that even though he was of the *pueblo*, he was much more than the *pueblo*. He narrated in detail how his humble social origins had not prevented him from becoming a successful businessman, politician, sportsman and lawyer. Because Bucaram came from humble origins, he shared the indignities and the opressions of the poor. Abdalá Bucaram is *el pueblo* because he, too, has suffered. He has been sued and incarcerated on phony charges, and poor people know the class bias of the justice system. The laws and jails are not for the rich. Thanks to his superior character and great manhood, Bucaram has sacrificed himself for the poor; and like many of them, he has become a martyr. In many speeches he said: "I paid my political dues, I was exiled, imprisoned, and sued." His suffering and dedication to the needs of the people transformed him into the self-proclaimed "leader of the poor." These two qualities — his sacrifices for the poor and his simultaneous membership in *el pueblo*, but also his superiority to most common people — transform a man of humble social origins into a person who deserved to become the president of Ecuador. That is why in his 1996 presidential campaign he said, "I have the right to the presidency of the republic."

Populist allegations of out-of-the-ordinariness in some cases have more than a kernel of truth. Evo Morales grew up in abject poverty in his rural Bolivian indigenous community. According to his own accounts, as a child he dreamed of the luxury of perhaps one day riding on a bus, and eating oranges and bananas. During his first months as president, giant propaganda was placed with the slogan "I am Evo." According to sociologist Fernando Mayorga, it meant that the leader could be any of us. Yet he is exceptional because he is the first indigenous to be president. Morales never imagined what he was going to become later in his life. His biography is linked to the struggles of the union of coca leaf growers. When he was elected to Congress he was promptly removed with accusations of have been a drug dealer, and later the U.S. embassy warned Bolivians not to vote for a drug trafficker as president. The leader of the coca growers was transformed into a martyr and victim of imperialism and politicians from the oligarchy.

Marco Garrido's ethnography explains how Joseph Estrada was considered to be out of the ordinary by his followers. In the case of Estrada, his daily acts more than his extraordinariness as a former movie star explain why the poor supported him, even though he was imprisoned for corruption and did not redistribute much income or wealth while in office. The poor in Manila, as in many developing cities, are stigmatized by elites as dirty squatters, and they know that politicians only visit their neighborhoods during election times. Contrary to other candidates, the poor interpreted Estrada's performances as authentic and sincere as he ate with them, greeted them warmly, and gave them symbolic and cultural recognition.

Charisma and Myths

Charismatic leaders invoke myths. Some are religiously inspired, others more secular. Feminist historian Marysa Navarro beautifully describes the myth of Eva Perón as the Mater Dolorosa in the following terms:

"Blond, pale, and beautiful, Evita was the incarnation of the Mediator, a Virgin-like figure who despite her origins, shared the perfection of the Father because of her closeness to him. Her mission was to love infinitely, give herself to others and 'burn her life' for others, a point made painfully literal when she fell sick with cancer and refused to interrupt her activities. She was the Blessed Mother, chosen by God to be near 'the leader of the new world: Perón.' She was the childless mother who became the Mother of all the descamisados, the Mater Dolorosa who 'sacrificed' her life so that the poor, the old, and the downtrodden could find some happiness."

The persona of Hugo Chávez symbolized the myths of Bolivar, the liberator, and of Jesus Christ, the Savior. His political movement, the new constitution and Venezuela were re-baptized as "Bolivarian." He was erected by his followers into the carrier of Bolívar's project of national and continental liberation. He asserted to be following the footsteps of the "true Bolívar, the Bolívar of the people, the revolutionary Bolívar." He even changed the old whitish images of Bolivar's representations. Chávez's Bolivar was portrayed with a brown skin color similar to his devotee's, regardless of the fact that the liberator came from a family of slave owners. To celebrate the tenth anniversary of his presidency, Chávez visited the tomb of Bolívar and asserted, "Ten years ago, Bolívar —embodied in the will of the people— came back to life."

Chávez constantly invoked "Jesus as 'my commander in chief' and as 'the Lord of Venezuela'." Chávez compared his leadership to Jesus Christ's. In 1999 he asserted, "true love for other human beings is measured by whether you can die for others; and here we are ready to die for others." His prophetic words of following Jesus' example of giving his life to liberate his people were dramatically manifested when Chávez compared his agony with cancer with the passion of Christ. During a religious service broadcast by national television during Holy Week in 2012, he prayed out loud:

"Give me life...Christ give me your crown of thorns. Give it to me that I bleed. Give me your cross...Give me life because I still need to do things for this people and motherland. Do not take me. Give me your cross, your thorns, your blood. I will carry them, but give me life. Christ my Lord. Amen."

His followers erected Chávez into a saint-like figure with the powers to heal. Psychoanalyst and writer Ana Teresa Torres in *La Herencia de la Tribu* narrates these two episodes. In 1999, an elderly woman grabbed him by the arm to beg "Chávez help me my son has paralysis." A crying young man stopped him outside the door of Caracas Cathedral and told him, "Chávez help me, I have two sons that are dying of hunger and I do not want to become a delinquent, save me from this inferno." After his death, his handpicked successor, Nicolás Maduro, consecrated Chávez into a secular saint. Mariana González Trejo's Ph.D. dissertation explains how Maduro buried Chávez in a newly built shrine, a pantheon that "symbolizes the renaissance of the homeland and the immeasurable life of the Eternal Commandant." His coffin has the inscription "Supreme Commander of the Bolivarian Revolution." And above his sarcophagus in the center there is a portrait of Bolívar the Father with one of Chávez his Son on its right and left sides.

Chávez was not the only populist who claimed to follow in the footsteps of national heroes.

General Juan Perón professed to be continuing the unfinished mission of General San Martín, who liberated Argentina from Spain. Perón's mission was to rid Argentina of imperialists and the oligarchy. Similarly, Jean Marie Le Pen claimed that he was the heir of Joan of Arc. Zúquete writes, "in the same way that Joan led France in fighting the decadence of the past, Le Pen will lead France in fighting decadence of the present."

Even though Silvio Berlusconi at times compared himself to Christ, saying that he was a "reluctant leader, forced to bear the cross or accept the bitter chalice of leading his people," his charisma was more secular. He emerged in politics after the Tangentopoli scandal that discredited the entire political class between 1993 and 1994, and which led to the collapse of the old parties. According to Carlo Ruzza and Stefano Fella in *Reinventing the Italian Right*, Berlusconi used the myth of the ingenuity of the Italian entrepreneur to claim that he was the best person to revive the Italian economy. He appealed to:

> "The average hard working Italian, who is not very political but anti-communist and holding traditional catholic and conservative values, who dreams of material success that would allow him/her to live the lifestyles portrayed on the Berlusconi-owned TV channels that are watched religiously by a laser swathe of the Italian population."

To cement the myth that he was an outsider and not a traditional politician, and that he was a man of the people, Berlusconi used crude misogynist remarks, and used his playboy image to represent male fantasies that he could have any woman he wanted. His vulgar gestures, Ruzza and Fella wrote, validated his leadership.

Donald Trump triumphed in two mythical and almost religious arenas of American capitalism: the business world and mass entertainment. From the beginning of his presidential campaign, Trump referred to his own extraordinariness. "We need a truly great leader now. We need a leader that wrote 'The Art of the Deal' ... We need somebody that can take the brand of the United States and make it great again." Billionaire Donald Trump flaunted his wealth; his name became a brand for skyscrapers, hotels, golf courses, casinos, steaks and other commodities; he owned the Miss Universe franchise; and with the TV show *The Apprentice* that he hosted for fourteen seasons, he became a media celebrity. People at his rallies told ethnographer Arlie Hochschild they were amazed to "be in the presence of such a man."

To Make America Great Again, he argued that what was needed was a successful businessman and popular culture impresario who was not corrupted by the deals of politicians and lobbyists. He stirred emotions, and was able to construct politics like a wrestling match between good, incarnated in his persona, and the crooked establishment, personified by Hillary Clinton. She was portrayed as the embodiment of all that was wrong with America, therefore, and without a proper trial Trump and his followers condemned her to prison, chanting at his rallies, "Lock her up!" Many proudly wore T-shirts or carried signs that read "Hillary for Prison." John Judis writes that Trump claimed "the establishment, the media, the special interests, the lobbyists, the big donors, they are all against me." His final campaign TV ads indicted the "failed and corrupt political establishment" for giving up America's sovereignty to global and greedy elites that brought "destruction to our factories." With images of the predominantly white crowds that attended his rallies, he concluded, "The only thing that can stop this corrupt machine is you. I am doing this for the people and for the movement."

5. Group of Donald Trump supporters on the USS Iowa battleship in San Pedro, California, adapting the slogan "Make American Great Again," which Trump used to seduce his followers in the 2016 presidential campaign.

The Charisma of Rhetoric

In *Economy and Society*, Weber wrote that stump speeches prioritize rhetoric over content and are "purely emotional." The rhetoric "has the same meaning as the street parades and festivals: to imbue the masses with the notion of the party's power and confidence in victory and, above all, to convince them of the leader's charismatic qualifications." Weber also differentiated between scientific and political speeches. He wrote, "the enterprise of the prophet is closer to that of the popular leader (demagogos) or the political publicist than that of the teacher."

Mass Politics

Elaborating on Weber's distinction, José Álvarez Junco explains in *The Emergence of Mass Politics* in Spain that because the goal of political speeches is to motivate people to act, well-reasoned arguments are less useful than emotional appeals. Political discourse "does not inform or explain but persuades and shapes attitudes." Populism is a Manichaean rhetoric that divides society in two antagonistic camps: the people versus the oligarchy. Mass meetings are the spaces where charismatic leadership is recognized through the repetition of a series of rituals. For example, in the 1940s

Colombian leader Jorge Gaitán closed all his rallies by shouting pueblo, and the masses responded "against the oligarchy." Populist discourses are collective creations. Leaders repeat successful words and slogans, and they respond to the accusations of their rivals. For instance, when the followers of five-time Ecuadorian president Velasco Ibarra were depicted as the mob, he responded: "yes this is the velasquista mob made up of artisans, women, peasants, working bodies, noble souls that are the heart of the nation. The mob is redeeming the fatherland from corruption."

Weber also argued: "it is the recognition on the part of those subject to authority which is decisive for the validity of charisma." Mass meetings are the arenas in which the populist leader is recognized and acclaimed by followers. With the repetition of songs, slogans and banners, mass meetings aim to create political identities or to at least differentiate the in-group from the out-group.

A former leader of the National Front Youth interviewed by Pedro Zúquete explains:

"As in religions, the greater gatherings keep alive the 'faith' of the militants: they notice that they are not alone in having their ideas, that the National Front is powerful, organized, gatherer. The speeches, in front of thousands of people, serve to give the watchwords, slogans that the militants will use to persuade people. It is exactly the same function as the Sunday Mass: The communion to bind together the believers, and the sermon to give instructions or explain some details of the doctrine... [The militants] can also personally meet the officials, shake their hands, and talk to them. For them it is a sort of reward. These gatherings give courage and will to fight to the militants, who go home highly motivated."

Despite innovative use of television to create media spectacles and social media like Twitter, Trump's campaign, like that of other populists, made ample use of mass rallies. Trump's rallies showed his followers, who for the most part were whites, that they were no longer a "besieged minority." A politician who claimed to represent their interests and identities finally addressed thousands like them. As Trump said, he was the candidate of "the forgotten men and women of this country," the white working- and middle-class. In *Strangers in Their Own Land*, Hochschild writes that to those "who attended his rallies, the event itself symbolizes a rising tide."

I studied the mass meetings, stump speeches and campaign trails of several elections in Ecuador. My ethnography of Abdalá Bucaram showed that his electoral strategy was based on the performance of political spectacles staged all over the country. These political spectacles combined the show of *el loco* (the crazy one), who sings and dances with the emotion of attending a concert to chant with familiar melodies. Through humor, music and mockery, he transformed mass political rallies into spectacles of transgression in which he challenged the elite's power and privileges. Bucaram's transgression was ambiguous. On the one hand, he questioned the social order when, for instance, he referred to ladies of high society as "a bunch of lazy old women that have never cooked or ironed." He contrasted what he labeled as the effeminate men of the oligarchy to the people's and his own virility. He portrayed working-class women as the standard-bearers of truthful womanhood, in contrast to the women of the oligarchy who do not work or take care of their children. On the other hand, he also accepted and strengthened the structural bases of domination. He believed in neoliberalism, professing that it would benefit the poor. He used misogynist and homophobic tropes to differentiate the truthful people from elites. Moreover, Bucaram's authoritarian appropriation of the people's will, which he claimed to embody, posed fundamental dangers to democracy.

Rafael Correa's campaign strategy in 2006 was also based on mass rallies, where common people were in close proximity to the candidate and sang along with him to revolutionary music of the 1960s and 1970s. Even though his music was retro, Correa's political rhetoric was innovative. Unlike the long and boring speeches of his rivals, Correa blended music and dance with speech-making. He spoke briefly, presenting a simple idea, music was played, and Correa and the crowd sang along to the campaign tunes and danced. When the music stopped, Correa spoke briefly again followed by music, songs and dance. These innovations allowed people to participate and brought feelings that Correa and his followers were part of a common political project, a "citizens' revolution" against the partyarchy. This was also a good strategy for young people, who get bored listening to speeches, and for television and YouTube viewers, who were presented only a snapshot of his rallies.

6. Crowds celebrate Macron's victory over Marine Le Pen at the Louvre Museum after the presidential elections. Paris (France), May 7, 2017.

Love is the link between leader and followers. Jean Marie Le Pen presented himself as the "patriot of love," and the National Front as a community of love. Bucaram said: "I am the crazy man who loves."

He loved his people, his nation, the only ones not deserving his love were those of the oligarchy, a flexible term that could include anybody who was critical or disloyal to him. Hugo Chávez always talked about how much he loved his people. In the 2009 campaign to change the constitution with a referendum to allow for his permanent re-election, the following reasons were given to vote for Chávez's proposal: "because Chávez loves us, and we have to repay his love; because Chávez loves us and will not harm us; because Chávez and us are one."

Most populist gatherings I attended in Latin America were fiestas to celebrate the leader and in which followers felt part of the same political community. For instance, when I attended Chávez's 2012 campaign in Caracas amid a tropical rain he danced with his people, who for the most part were poor and non-white and had gathered by the thousands in downtown Caracas. Much like what Garrido describes about the poor in Manila, the words and performance of leaders such as Chávez or Bucaram were possibly discussed in the neighborhoods where the poor live. In "Why the Poor Support Populism" Garrido wrote, "The segregation of the urban poor in slum areas facilitates conversations among people occupying a similar social position. When the urban poor talk about Estrada, being similarly predisposed, they tend to corroborate one another's accounts. Social corroboration invests belief with authority. Belief grows beyond individual and household opinion and takes on the proportion of a collective representation, that is, it becomes a social fact."

Because the aim of populist meetings is to reinforce the identity of the people against its enemies, there was always the possibility of violence. For instance, Bucaram claimed that his rivals would try to assassinate him and his followers, and Chávez's male followers displayed their masculinity by aggressively riding their motorcycles. Yet in the U.S., the performance of acts of violence is also used to generate collective identities. American populists like George Wallace and Trump used their mass meetings as spaces to perform violence to generate in-group solidarity. Joseph Lowndes writes, "Violent antagonism played a particularly strong role in the case of George Wallace, the threat, anticipation and performance of which was central to his image and success." Grattan in *Populism's Power* sustains that "Tea Partiers are notorious, in particular for their performance of anger and fear." Their populism is based on an existential threat, "they are afraid of losing their 'way of life' and the promise of white, male, Christian privilege that comes with it." Their anger leads them to action, to fight to "take back the country."

Similarly, Trump used verbal and physical violence to mark frontiers between his white people and the out groups, and to arouse angry passions at his rallies. Arlie Hochschild reports some of Trump's words about what to do with those protesting at his rallies: "I'd like to punch him in the face." "Knock the crap out of him, would you? I promise you I will pay the legal fees." Timothy Snyder narrates in his volume *On Tyranny* the following incident. While at a campaign rally, Trump pointing to a critic shouted:

> "'There is a remnant left over there. Maybe get the remnant out. Get the remnant out.' The crowd, taking its cue, then tried to root out other people who might be dissenters, all the while crying USA. The candidate interjected 'isn't this more fun than a regular boring rally?'"

The Body of the Leader

Weber wrote that charismatic leaders are "bearers of specific gifts of the body and mind that were considered 'supernatural' (in the sense that not everybody could have access to them)." The leaders claim their superiority because of naturally endowed powers, revolutionary ideas or the capacity to become the center of the social order. It seems that Hugo Chávez and Rafael Correa never slept during their long presidential tenures. They called their advisors and ministers at any time of the night, started their days very early and finished late at night, and claimed that they were always working to liberate their people. Orçun Selçuk writes in "Strong Presidents and Weak Institutions: Populism in Turkey, Venezuela and

Ecuador" that Recep Tayyip Erdogan was considered by his followers as 'the Chief ' (*Reis*) referring to his paternalistic leadership, 'the Tall Man' (*Uzun Adam*) referring to his height, 'the Conqueror of Davos' (*Davos Fatihi*) referring to his bold stance against Israel during the 2009 World Economic Forum, and 'the Master' (*Usta*) referring to his political skills. Rafael Correa disregarded neoliberal economists as accountants, and argued that he was the only economist who knew how to lead the hyper-modernization of Ecuador. Trump constantly boasts the he is the ultimate "dealmaker." He also claims that his critics, especially if they are women or people of color, are dumb, a dummy or a dog, as when he referred to his former protégé and advisor Omarosa Manigault Newman.

Juan Perón and Hugo Chávez created new political ideologies to transcend the failures of both Communism and capitalist liberal democracies. Justicialism in the 1950s and twenty-first century Socialism were advocated as the new panaceas for their nations, and these leaders aimed to export their models of political and socioeconomic change to Latin America and worldwide.

The body of the leader —which is no other than the body of the people struggling for its liberation— became omnipresent. Sociologist Juan José Sebreli, in his essay on Argentinean myths, explained that for seven years Eva Perón was present everywhere. Her face was on millions of billboards in streets and in stores, the state radio broadcasted her speeches daily, and she had a prominent role in the weekly news shown in all Argentinean movie theaters. In the same way, Hugo Chávez and Rafael Correa put their images or slogans from their regimes in visible spots along highways and cities. They used mandatory TV and radio messages to constantly broadcast their images and to make their bodies seen in newspapers, television and on social media, as they were constantly on Twitter and Facebook.

Similarly Donald Trump's image is everywhere at all times. Pundits are constantly discussing and analyzing his latest tweet. The obsessive needs of television for politics as entertainment meets with the compulsive need of the populist to become a permanent feature in citizens' everyday lives.

Ambivalence of Populist Politics

Because the body of the leader is everywhere and his aim is to confront rivals and to transform politics into Schmittian struggles between irreconcilable camps, his body is a site of antagonistic confrontation. Latin American societies that overvalue whiteness were polarized by discussions about the color of skin and the non-white features of populist leaders. Historian Herbert Braun argues that Colombian populist Jorge Eliécer Gaitán in the

1940s presented his physical appearance as a challenge to the political norms of white, elite-run restricted democracy. His teeth were seen by elites as symbols of animal aggression, his dark skin represented what white elites referred to as the feared *malicia indígena* (Indian wickedness). In sum, the image of "*el negro Gaitán*" was seen as a threat to "decent society." Yet it pervaded the press, electoral posters and caricatures.

In addition, in contrast to the cleanliness and serenity of the politicians in the Conservative and Liberal establishment, during his speeches Gaitán sweated, shouted and growled. Similarly, white and elite Venezuelans were repelled by Chávez's body, and especially by the visibility of his poor and non-white supporters. They called Chávez a monkey and made fun of his supporters' poor dental health. Evo Morales's *chompa* (sweater) and hairstyle were discussed in the Bolivian media as not fit for a head of state. Similarly, the middle-class focused on Estrada's persona as the subject of an entire class of "Erap jokes" having to do with his alleged dim-wittedness, his infidelities and his inarticulacy.

As in a play of mirror images, followers viewed favorably what elites considered as threats and denigrations for decent society. Hillary Clinton's remark that Trump's supporters were a "basket of deplorables" backfired and emboldened the millionaire's base of support. Some populists matched their words with deeds. Evo Morales transformed Bolivia's public sphere from mono-cultural mestizo to multiethnic and multicultural, with indigenous people serving in the government and in the legislature.

Some populists failed to be convincing as the embodiment of popular culture. Abdalá Bucaram represented himself as the leader of the poor. The upper middle-class and elites read his actions and performances as the personification of barbarism. For instance, Bucaram explained his shows of dancing and singing at his public meetings and as president on television by comparing himself to Argentinean president Carlos Menem, who sang tangos, and to president Bill Clinton, who played the saxophone. He also asked his critics: "What man has not charmed a woman by singing a serenade?" Now, using Los Iracundos, the pop group with which he captivated his wife, Bucaram was attempting to seduce the Ecuadorian people. His opponents had a different reading. For instance, the well-respected journalist Francisco Febres Cordero wrote: "The singer [Bucaram] gathered all the filth from the most pestilent sewers to throw it at the face of his audience with no other intention than to perform a spectacle." When thousands marched against Bucaram, many explained that he had debased the presidency with his vulgar performances. Bucaram became the repugnant other and was overthrown by Congress with the rationale that he was crazy, alas without medical proof of his alleged mental incapacity to govern.

The leader offers his body to be touched by followers. Estrada, Trump, Chávez, Correa and Morales constantly toured their nations and met, talked and were touched by common people. Bucaram imitated the televangelist style of praising the Lord with music, songs and participation by the people. His style also simulated the charismatic Pentecostal leaders who go into trances while adoring God. This is why he jumped off the platform after each speech and walked through the masses. The audience tried to touch their leader who, like Christ, touched the people to heal and redeem them.

Populists also use their bodies to brag about their hyper-masculinities. Abdalá Bucaram said that one of his rivals had watery sperm, and of another that he had no balls. Like Bucaram, Trump bragged about the size of his genitalia and his masculine superiority manifested in his power to grab any desirable women, pointing out that middle-aged Hillary Clinton was undesirable. Benjamin Moffitt writes that Berlusconi "boasted of having sex with up to eight women a night, and has been embroiled in a number of scandals involving 'bunga' parties with prostitutes."

Populist leaders use their personal success in business, the media, mass culture, the military or sports to show their extraordinariness. Trump, Berlusconi and Shinawatra used their successes in the business world to claim their superiority. Former Philippine actor Joseph Estrada used his cinematographic roles as a Robin Hood-like character to claim to be the benefactor of the poor. Fernando Collor used his success in the world of sports. Perón and Chávez presented themselves as brilliant military men who sacrificed their military careers for their nations. Jean Marie Le Pen said that France is at war, and formed battalions of militants of the National Front. Perón referred to his followers as Peronist soldiers, and Chávez organized his supporters in battalions and squads for epic wars against imperialism.

The image most populist leaders share is their claim to be the fathers of their homelands. Getulio Vargas claimed to be "the father of the poor," while Lázaro Cárdenas was "tata Lázaro." During his campaign, Trump represented the image of a good father and surrounded himself with his children. Later, he named his daughter and son-in-law political advisers with almost unrestricted access to the White House. His image of a millionaire good father symbolically promised to gather under his wise paternal tutelage all of those who uncritically accepted his wisdom. The father metaphor, as Karen Kampwirth wrote in *Gender and Populism in Latin America*, "turns citizens into permanent children. It turns a politician into someone who understands the interests of citizens —even when they do not— and who may punish wayward children who fail to recognize their wisdom." The job of a father never ends, and populists from Perón to Chávez and Morales attempted to stay in power indefinitely.

Female populist leaders are not as vulgar, yet Moffitt describes how Pauline Hanson in Australia appeared in a swimsuit while washing cars in the reality television show *Celebrity Apprentice*, and Sarah Palin "coquettishly winked during her speeches." Yet, as he argued, they combine these images of femininity with their role as mothers. Hanson even said: "The Australian people are my children," and Palin called herself a "Mama Grizzly."

The Body of the People

Populists construct the people as a homogenous body with one will and interest that is only that of the leader. A diverse population with distinct interests, demands and proposals is homogenized into a single unitary body. The *pars pro toto* dynamic of populism symbolically expels those who do not agree with the leader from the people and the nation. Even disloyal fellow travelers can become enemies. The image of the people of populism is quite different from the democratic body of the people. Building on Kantorowicz's *The King's Two Bodies*, Claude Lefort showed the different images of the body of the people in monarchies, democracies and totalitarian regimes. According to Kantarowicz, the King, like God, was "omnipresent, for in himself he constituted the 'body politic' over which he ruled. But like his son whom God sent to redeem mankind, he was man as well as God; he had a 'body natural' as well as his body politic, and the two were inseparable like the persons of the Trinity." The king's body was mortal and time-bound, as well as immortal and eternal. It was imagined as individual as well as collective. Once the immortal body of the king and the body of the politic were decapitated during the revolutions of the 18th century, the space occupied by the religious political body of the king was opened up. Claude Lefort wrote that power was no longer linked to a body. "Power appears as an empty place and those who exercise it as merely mortals who occupy it only temporarily or who could install themselves in it only by force or cunning." In a democracy, the will of the majority is not the same as the will of the people as a whole. The people of today are not necessarily the people of tomorrow, as the power of today is not the power of tomorrow. Under democracy the image of the people "remains indeterminate" and cannot be embodied in an individual like a King or a leader regardless of how popular she is.

In *The Rise of Global Populism*, Benjamin Moffitt writes that populism is an attempt "to re-embody the body politic, to suture the head back on the corpse. And provide unity in the name of the people through the leader." It aims to get rid of the uncertainties of democratic politics by naming a leader as the embodiment of the people and nation. Yet this attempt is different from fascism, which abolished democracy altogether. As Enrique Peruzzotti maintains, the vote for populists is the only legitimate tool to legitimate getting to power, therefore democratic uncertainty is not fully abolished. Andrew Arato wrote that populism filled the open space of democracy, yet in contrast to fascism and other totalitarianisms did not entirely obliterate it. Hence populists often failed in their attempt to build homogenous peoples under their leadership.

The two most paradigmatic populist regimes, those of Perón and Chávez, failed to create Peronist or Bolivarian national populist citizens. Their policies were resisted by intellectuals, journalists, middle-class sectors, social movement leaders, organizations of civil society, some leftist parties and by politicians from the opposition. Their attempts to be the only voice of the people were also contested by sectors of their coalitions, and by sympathetic social movements that used the opening up of the political system to push for their autonomous demands. Peronist workers and many Bolivarian organizations did not succumb to the will of their leaders, but rather strategically supported their policies and pushed these leaders to fulfill their democratizing and redistributive promises.

Even though Peronism and Chavism were not able to create homogeneous national communities, they polarized their nations into two antagonistic and irreconcilable camps. Populists and their detractors saw each other not as democratic adversaries, but as enemies. The opposition, which felt marginalized and with little opportunities to get back into power using democratic institutions, plotted military coups against Perón and Chávez. Populists, for their part, excluded those who did not uncritically accept Perón or Chávez as the only and truthful voice of the people. They were branded as enemies of the populist leader, the people and the nation.

The Revolutionary and Autocratic Perils of Charisma and Populism

Weber wrote: "charisma is indeed the specifically creative revolutionary force of history." Yet he had ambivalences about the democratizing effects of charisma, and recognized the dangers of charisma without the mediations of political parties and parliamentary institutions. In the absence of parties and democratic institutions that socialize leaders into the politics of democratic compromise Weber wrote, "the leader (demagogue) rules by virtue of devotion and trust which his political followers have in him personally."

Populists have historically destroyed limited democracies and included those excluded on the condition that they accept their leadership. Its inclusionary credentials, as will be shown in Chapter 4, worked better in democracies that were increasing the size of the electorate, and in conditions of acute inequalities and undemocratic privileges. Yet under populism, elections were lived as plebiscites on the leader. Politics was transformed into moral-religious struggles, infringing upon the plurality of opinions and interest of complex societies. Plebiscites transformed politics into confrontations between two antagonistic camps. Because populists saw democratic adversaries as enemies of the people, populist regimes selectively limited the rights of the opposition to express different points of view. They did not always respect the rule of law or the notion of accountability.

Weber argued that charisma revolutionizes men from within. Populist identities generated by charismatic movements can transform the attitudes and worldviews of followers. To be a Peronist, a Chavista or perhaps a Trumpist means to have a vision of politics and society based on a Manichaean struggle between the people and its enemies in which all conflicts are dramatized as antagonistic confrontations between two camps. Peronist and Chavista identities could last over time because these movements institutionalized charisma into parties and organizations of civil society. When charisma was not routinized in parties or organizations of civil society, serial populism emerged. After the breakdown of political parties in Ecuador or Peru, a series of populist leaders whose rule did not last over time succeeded each other in office.

The relationships between charismatic populist leaders and liberal democracy are complex. Populists incorporate excluded groups that are humiliated by elites. Populism is a politics of cultural and symbolic recognition. Paraphrasing Jacques Rancière, "it consists in making what was unseen visible, in making what was audible as mere noise heard as speech." Those who are excluded and stigmatized with categories such as "the poor," "the informal" and "the marginal" become "the people" conceived as the incarnation of all virtue. And those who constantly humiliate them become the hideous elites. Populists also materially include the excluded by redistributing favors and privileges to supporters.

Despite its democratizing effects, populism is based on what Weber described as plebiscitary acclamation. In the absence of parties and solid institutions, populism can open the door for a perception of the exercise of political power as a possession rather than as occupancy. In contrast to politicians who work on the premise that they will not always remain in power, populists concentrate power and reduce institutional spaces for the opposition under the assumption that their government will stay in power until the jobs of transforming the state and society are done.

Chapter 3

How Leaders are Linked with their Followers

This chapter analyzes different links between leaders and followers. It distinguishes between clientelism, populist organizations and the media. Populist followers are not irrational masses in a state of anomie, as earlier approaches based on mass society theory assumed. Nor are populist appeals reduced to the manipulation of the media for irrational audiences. Populist followers are organized at least in clientelist networks that exchange political support for access to goods and services. There are different types of populist organizations. Some are grassroots, such as those created by the Tea Party, The Five Star

Movement, The Northern League or Podemos. Other organizations, like Chávez's Bolivarian groups, were formed from the top down. Populist associations are part of civil society, and populism thrives in democratic public spheres. Yet as Andrew Arato and Jean Cohen write, "populism is in but not of civil society." It flourishes in civil society but its logic is "antithetical to the underlying principles of civil society." Populist organizations that are, for the most part, anti-pluralist and do not foster solidarity with other organizations undermine civil society's open, plural, inclusive and democracy-enhancing features. Similarly, populists demand the democratization of the media, but when in power aim to control and censure it to make the voice of the leader the only truthful and authorized voice of the people.

Clientelism

Latin American populist parties are organized through formal bureaucratic party networks and clientelist informal networks that distribute resources, information and jobs. The poor vote instrumentally for the candidate with the best capacity to deliver goods and services. In many Latin American, Asian and African nations, the poor live under conditions of material and legal deprivation and in environments of dire violence and insecurity. Because their constitutionally prescribed civil rights are not always respected, the poor rely on politicians and their networks of brokers to have access to a bed in a public hospital or a job. Brokers are the intermediaries between politicians and poor people. They hoard information and resources and are connected to wider networks and cliques of politicians and state officials. Formal bureaucratic rules work together with personalist cliques and networks of friends who dispense "favors," including corruption. Because the poor can choose to leave a broker and join a different network, brokers' positions are unstable, and the poor cannot be viewed as a manipulated and captive voting base. The poor can exit a network, they can also choose to not vote as the broker requested, or might feel compelled to repay a favor to the broker. The unreliable nature of political support gives certain advantages to the poor. For the system of exchanges to work, politicians have to deliver at least some resources.

Clientelism played an important role in how political parties in Zambia delivered to their constituencies. Alastair Fraser in his article "Post-populism in Zambia: Michael Sata's rise, demise and legacy" explains, "middlemen mobilize voters and connect them to political celebrities. They also often play a role in organizing the distribution of everyday life opportunities (plots of land, market stalls and work)." Populist Michael Sata told his supporters to accept the gifts from the Movement for Multi-party Democracy (MMD), but to vote for him and his candidates.

Clientele Networks

Like other political parties, populists exchange services for votes. But in addition to offering material rewards, populist exchanges go together with a discourse that portrays common people as the essence of the nation. In *Poor People's Politics*, Javier Auyero argues that the resilience of Peronism among the poor, for example, was partially explained by the informal and clientelist networks of the Peronist Party, who in addition to delivering material resources to the poor recreated political and cultural identities. Clientelist exchanges are based on performances. Auyero argues that brokers must act in accord with the expectations of their constituents. They distribute goods "not as a bribe, but as a gift bestowed out of a great love for the people."

Populist exchanges are also based on etiquette. The gifts have to appear as sincere and not as crude tools to get votes. Sometimes the poor, such as in Zambia, accept gifts and vote for other candidates of their choice. In other cases, politicians who appear out of the blue with gifts in neighborhoods are labeled as manipulators.

Kurt Weyland wrongly argues that one of populism's definitional traits is the direct appeal of a leader to disorganized followers. Perhaps the persistence of views of disorganized followers, which populated Weyland's and mass society approaches, reflect dominant views of populism as extraordinary phenomena. If normal politics is based on formal organizations like parties and unions, rapid social change, crises and other social breakdowns that supposedly lay at the roots of populism produce disorganization. Without denying that populism sometimes emerges in conditions of crisis, populism also arises in normal times, and in some nations is a recurrent feature of politics.

Ethnographic research on the strategies of survival and politics of the poor illustrate high levels of organization and strategic capacities to negotiate with the state and political parties. Because many of the poor illegally occupy land to build houses, and/or sell in the streets breaking city ordinances, they live in conditions of marginalization and on the border of illegalities. Organization is hence a necessity. Land invaders must divide land into lots. Street vendors must at least tacitly recognize the 'right' of others to specific locations, as well as to cooperate in building their market zone. Organization also allows negotiating the process of regulation with the state. Bureaucrats also promote organization because it is easier to negotiate with a recognized representative of a group than with a wide array of self-described leaders.

Populist Organizations

Some organizations are grassroots, while leaders create others from the top-down. Right-wing populist parties in Europe foster a sense of community by creating what sociologist Carlo Ruzza in his chapter in *The Routledge Handbook of Populism* called "populist civil society associations." These were formed in the name of "an undifferentiated, self-evident, and self-justified category of the people" who faced enemies defined in essentialist terms. Ruzza distinguishes between populist-xenophobic associations and nationalist-territorial groups. The former define the people and its enemies with racial categories, the latter with culturally essentialist categories. Examples of xenophobic association are neo-Nazi groups and the associations of the French National Rally. The Northern League, which recently changed its name to The League, constructed territorial-related populist associations such as language schools, hunters, drivers and hiker associations, and different Padonian groups (from the Padonia Vally of Po, Italy) for women, boy scouts and welfare groups.

These populist associations are examples of bonding social capital. They create strong identities, a sense of community, and clear boundaries between them and us. Members of these associations and groups only relate to like-minded individuals, are exclusionary and disdain pluralism. These organizations and associations, in sum, do not bridge social capital; instead, they undermine it.

Tea Party organizations are made up of relatively well-educated, middle-aged, white Americans. Conservatives and libertarians coexist in these organizations. Skocpol and Williamson in *The Tea*

Party and the Remaking of Republican Conservatism
note a "sharp bifurcation between generous, tolerant
interaction within the group, and an almost total
lack of empathy or sympathy for fellow Americans
beyond the group." The organizations of the Tea
Party are insular, and despise pluralism. They
dismiss organized African American and Latino
groups as threats to the nation, and Democratic
Party and liberal organizations are portrayed
as unpatriotic. Their insularity is magnified by
their reliance on Fox News and its nightmarish
representation of the U.S. as a nation where "illegal
immigrants, criminals, and badly behaving people
of color are overrunning America."

Laura Grattan explains that when the Tea Party
"was at its height, some two hundred thousand
people took part in regular, face-to-face community
organizing through up to one thousand active groups
across the country." According to Skocpol and
Williamson, Tea Partiers tend to be "Republican,
white, male, married, and older than 45." Their core
base is made up of economically better-off and better-
educated sectors than most Americans. Also, they
are mostly evangelical Protestants. An intermediate
circle of active supporters and passive sympathizers
surround a core base of activists. Women, writes
Robert Horwitz in his volume *America's Right*, have
a prominent and visible leadership at the local level.
Like other right-wing populists, Tea Parties are
opposed to liberal and cosmopolitan government

officials above and to dependents mostly of color below. They feel themselves to be victims of an unjust system that has robbed them of the fruits of their labor through excessive taxation. They are opposed to illegal immigration, arguing that illegals are "freeloaders who are draining public coffers." They believe that "racial minorities are held back by their own personal failings." They fear and hate Islam, considered a religion that espouses terrorism. Yet they do not use openly racist terms, but code words to refer to African Americans. They see themselves as true patriotic Americans, and consider it a waste of time to find compromises with Democrats. Their foreign policy views according to Horwitz are isolationist, and they have an aversion to international organizations.

Populist organizations like the Tea Party or The League do not foster the politics of a plural and democratic civil society. Their insularity does not allow them to build links with other organizations, and their notion that they and only they constitute the true people leads to the autocratic exclusion of those considered to be the ultimate Other. Grattan concludes that the Tea Party is dangerous for democracy because they narrow citizenship rights, restrict access to social services, and support austerity and tax measures that enhance the ultra-rich.

In "Populism, Political Conflict, and Grassroots Organization In Latin America," Kenneth Roberts argues that populist leaders create organizations when their confrontations with the oligarchy are about politics, economics and culture. Populist polarization encourages populists to build long-lasting organizations in civil society. When the level of confrontation against the elite is not acute and populists are demanding only political transformations, they do not really have to organize their followers into parties or in civil society. José María Velasco Ibarra and Alberto Fujimori, who only challenged the political power of elites, created temporary organizations. In contrast Perón and Chávez, who created deep political and socioeconomic cleavages, built strong organizations to confront the economic, symbolic and political power of elites.

Organizations created by Chávez's government illustrate the tension between the autonomous demands of followers, who use the openings created by populism to present their own demands, and their subordination to a charismatic leader. In June 2001, President Chávez encouraged the formation of Bolivarian Circles. These were small groups of seven to fifteen people, which were intended to study the ideology of Bolivarianism, discuss local issues and defend the revolution. Bolivarian Circles had approximately 2.2 million members and had an active role in the massive demonstrations rescuing President Chávez when he was temporarily removed from office in an April 2002 coup d'état. According to Hawkins, Bolivarian Circles did constitute forms of participation for poor people, yet they often worked as patronage networks to transfer resources to neighborhoods where the president had supporters.

Communal Councils were conceived as institutions to promote popular power, and were seen as the foundation for the future establishment of a direct and pyramidal socialist democracy. Studies of communal councils differ in their evaluation of how many people in the community participated. Using the AmericasBarometer survey of 2007, Kirk Hawkins concludes that 35.5% of the adult population participates in Communal Councils, an exceptionally high figure of about 8 million participants. Yet results based on ethnographic research show lower levels of participation. Margarita Lopez Maya reports, "out of the 350 or 400 families that made a communal council in Caracas no more than fifteen people actively participate." Most of these are women who had previous experiences of participation. Communal Councils worked closely with the Barrio Nuevo Tricolor project of the armed forces. Through this mission, the military established military garrisons in poor neighborhoods to work on social projects, to give temporary work, and to provide a free lunch to unemployed young people. Chávez argued that the people and the armed forces needed to be united under his leadership to transform social, economic and moral structures, preserving national independence. However, the military presence in the everyday life of the poor posed the threats of militarization and of social and political control. Critics and supporters of the Bolivarian Revolution agreed that Communal Councils presented the same problems as the Bolivarian Circles, namely the persistence of clientelism in the exchange of social services for political support, and a charismatic style of rule that neutralizes or prevents autonomous grassroots inputs.

Bolivarian Circles and Communal Councils may have experienced problems of autonomy because they were created from above to promote Chávez's Bolivarian revolution. Other institutions, such as the Urban Land Committees and Technical Water Roundtables, for example, accepted more autonomous grassroots inputs and were more pluralist. The government gave squatter settlements collective titles to land on which precarious self-built dwellings were situated. Through this process, explains D.L. Raby in *Democracy and Revolution*, "the community forms an urban land committee to administer its new collective property and to undertake and demand support for material improvements such as water, sewerage and electricity services or road paving." Similarly, local water committees "arrange the distribution of water between neighboring communities which share the same water mains." Nevertheless, Urban Land and Water Committees lacked autonomy from the charismatic leader, as Chávez was the guiding force for these institutions.

As Kirk Hawkins showed in *Venezuela's Chavismo and Populism*, Bolivarian organizations were based on low levels of institutionalization. Chávez set their agendas and strategies, and it was difficult to build identities that differed from the image of the people as constructed by the leader. Bolivarian organizations were based on insularity, as they did not promote solidarity with similar organizations in civil society. They did not value pluralism because they adopted the idea of the people as an undifferentiated and homogeneous whole. Hence the people could only be organized under organizations loyal to Chávez. Yet sometimes common people used populist organizations and the rhetorical claim that they are the true nation to present their own demands. In contexts of profound political polarization, like those experienced in Venezuela under Chávez, populist organizations fostered loyalties and powerful political identities that partially explain the longevity of chavismo after his death.

The Mass Media

In *The Rise of Global Populism*, Benjamin Moffitt writes that "media processes need to be put at the center of our thinking about contemporary populism," and further maintains that populism is "the media-political form par excellence at this particular historical conjunction." Populism blurs the line between politics and entertainment. It also questions who has the power to deliver information and to control communication.

The Media: Populism and Entertainment

Populists were media innovators who politicized emotions to convey their anti-elite messages. In the 1940s and 50s, Eva Perón, who made a career in radio soap operas and as a movie actress, used the radio to communicate with her followers, transforming politics into a melodrama. Marysa Navarro explains, "Her scenarios never changed and her characters were stereotyped by the same adjectives: Perón was always 'glorious,' the people 'marvelous,' the oligarchy *egoísta y vende patria* [selfish and corrupt], and she was a 'humble' or 'weak' woman, 'burning her life for them' so that social justice could be achieved, *cueste lo que cueste y caiga quien caiga* [at whatever cost and regardless of the consequences]."

The rise of television further contributed to blurring the lines between politics and entertainment. According to Benjamin Moffitt, populist performative style and the media's logic are complementary. Populists' appeal to the people versus the elite "plays into the media's logic of dramatization, polarization and prioritization of conflicts." The personalization of politics in a leader is "in line with the media's logic of personalization, stereotypisation and emotionalisation; while its focus on crises plays into the media's tendency of intensification and simplification."

7. **Stamp printed in Argentina reflecting the myth of Eva Peron devoted to her people.**

In the 1990s, scholars argued that television transformed politics based on reason into media-politics based on melodrama. Giovanni Sartori sustained that television personalizes politics, presents politics as a spectacle, and is based on emotional appeals rather than the rational discussion of ideologies that characterized liberal parliamentary democracies. Populism, Sartori argued, has become telepopulism. For Pierre-André Taguieff it is a form of "video demagogy; the demagogue acts on his audience by letting himself be seen more than understood." As a result, "citizens are reduced to spectators, mere consumers of spectacles." Yoram Peri in *Telepopulism: Media and Politics in Israel* argued that the logic of television contributed to the personalization of politics in Israel, and gave priority to emotions over rational arguments. "The central place once occupied by party platforms, values and ideologies, and specially the candidate's political plans, was replaced by the personal characteristics of the political actors." Analyzing president Carlos Menem of Argentina, cultural critic Beatriz Sarlo wrote, "politics in the mass media is subordinated to the laws that regulate audiovisual flow: high impact, large quantities of undifferentiated visual information, and arbitrary binary syntax that is better suited to a matinee melodrama than to the political arena."

Carlo Ruzza and Stefano Fella in *Reinventing the Italian Right* rightly argued, "One needs to be careful in explaining political behavior with reference to television. While media strategies are increasingly and indisputably a major factor in politics their impact should be contextualized." Even though television became one of the main venues used by populists to win elections, it was not the only reason behind their rise to power. Some populists, like Alberto Fujimori in 1990 in Peru or Abdalá Bucaram in 1996, won presidential elections despite opposition from the media, and having less time on the air to broadcast their messages. By contrast, in Italy the media became an important site of political participation and identity. In the 1980s and 90s media entrepreneur Silvio Berlusconi and comedian Beppe Grillo used television to communicate with their followers. In the following decades, Grillo criticized television and used the web to communicate with his constituencies. Grillo's success is explained by his creative use of new media, like the web, with traditional electoral techniques such as mass meetings and personal contacts with citizens. Similarly, Podemos used the web and alternative television shows distributed by YouTube, voted for party platforms online, used grassroots organizations like the Podemos circles and staged mass demonstrations.

The Tea Party benefited from the deregulation of U.S. media that allowed for evangelists to create their own media venues, and the emergence of cable television, particularly Fox News. Journalist Alexander Stille explains that Fox News began operating in 1995 and transformed the news. They produced inexpensive in-studio programs, and to keep people from changing channels they used provocative content: "Bill O'Really pistol-whipping and cutting the mike of his guests or Glenn Beck spinning his bizarre apocalyptic conspiracy webs." In his volume *America's Right*, Robert Horwitz explains how "Fox News gave extensive coverage to Tea Party events even prior to the event themselves" functioning as recruiters as well as cheerleaders." The Tea Party had their own media and did not have to "rely, as social movements did previously, on their treatment by 'mainstream media' wedded in conventional, professional notions of newsworthiness, objectivity, balance, and the like." Olivier Jutel in *The Routledge*

Handbook of Global Populism writes, "The ideal *Fox News* viewer is not simply an audience member but an active prosumer that watches *Fox* as part of a broader movement logic associated with other acts of consumption that bolster the conservative media sphere. The rise of the Tea Party was critical in reinforcing *Fox* as a conservative lifestyle brand during the Obama presidency." Fox entertains their audience with outrageous images and ideas that produce pleasure and generate conservative worldviews and agendas. Fox News and other conservative media venues on the Internet have not displaced professional journalism, yet they have created information niches that are the main or only source of news for their constituencies. They have also influenced other news venues to cover the events that they consider to be crucial. This leads to a cycle of news spinning as mainstream media invite conservatives to present their points of view, and to their critics to respond and then further rounds of response.

Fox News became the official voice and broadcaster of Trump's administration. He did not need to create a state channel; Fox, whose executives have prominent positions in his administration, in practice functions like Chávez's or Correa's state television. *The New York Times* reported on July 24, 2018, that Trump enacted a rule "that the White House entourage begin each trip tuned to Fox — his preferred network over what he considers the 'fake news' CNN." He also encouraged supporters to only believe in his words and in Fox News. Trump said in a mass rally in Kansas City Missouri: "stick with us. Don't believe the crap you see from these people, the fake news... What you are seeing and what you are reading is not what is happening." Fox News is controlling political debates because other media venues respond to Trump's words on this network.

Under Trump's administration, politics and entertainment merged, transforming his administration into a media spectacle. The president is constantly struggling against enemies. According to the president, his entourage, as in a soap opera or on reality TV, are conspiring and betraying him. His fights with his former lawyers, advisors and collaborators, while entertaining the public, put Trump at the center of the social order. His images, tweets, words and gestures dominate the media, causing enjoyment or shock on audiences. Some claim that these spectacles are smoke screens that hide how he is ruling in the interest of millionaires. Yet Trump is the show, and as long as he remains the lead story for journalists and pundits, he will continue to be the most important topic of debates and conversations.

Wars Against the Media

Donald Trump is not the only populist at war with the media. Like other populists, he despises critical and watchdog journalism, yet looks to the mainstream media to deliver his messages and seeks to construct media events where he becomes the center of the social order. While some populists, such as Abdalá Bucaram, lost their wars with the media, which contributed to taking him out of power, others like Rafael Correa won his war, closing critical media venues, suing journalists and media owners, and broadcasting his words as the only truth for ten long years.

Abdalá Bucaram staged his governmental actions as a televised show that represented power as the dramatization of nonpolitical spaces of popular culture, such as football and mass entertainment. Bucaram, a former athlete who had participated in the Munich Olympics, became president of Barcelona, Guayaquil's most important soccer team. He recorded a CD, *El loco que ama* (The crazy one who loves), with the pop group Los Iracundos and presented it on national television. He auctioned off his mustache for a million dollars for charity on a televised show where he danced with bleached-blonde models and told jokes. Lorena Bobbit, the Ecuadorian woman who gained notoriety by cutting off her abusive American Marine husband's penis, was his honorary guest.

By staging his triumphs in two valued realms of mass culture, Bucaram was representing common people's dreams of success and social mobility: to play soccer with well-known stars or to become a TV show personality. Using constant media exposure, he attempted to construct his persona as the central political event. His image as a winner in nonpolitical spheres like sports arenas and his transformation into a singer and television star were constantly broadcast into people's homes. He was acting on television for the public, while simultaneously transforming the meaning of public political debates. The discussion of his personal life, his dreams and televised performances became as important as the debates about his policies. That is why his opinions on which soccer players should be hired by Barcelona were announced simultaneously with his defense of his economic program. This constant media exposure also transformed the figure of the president. Instead of following the conventions of a rational bureaucratic ruler, he showed that even though he was the leader of the nation, he was like the common people. He did not follow the rules and protocols expected of a president. He refused to live in Quito's Presidential Palace because he claimed that it was haunted. He preferred to stay in expensive hotels during his short visits to Quito, and to govern from his home in Guayaquil.

Even the language he used contrasted with the words of rational bureaucratic government. He used commonsense expressions and the language of the street, or what Bakhtin calls "marketplace speech and gesture." By using these colloquialisms, he sought to create an atmosphere of frankness between the president and his followers and to validate what he considered the traits of popular culture. Yet his autocratic appropriation of the meanings of popular culture, understood as vulgarities, was resisted not only by elites but also by organized groups such as workers unions or indigenous organizations.

Bucaram was elected despite the opposition of most newspaper editorials. They questioned his unorthodox and flamboyant style, his authoritarian appropriation of the people's will, and the impossibility of having dialogues in which different opinions could be voiced. Bucaram forced journalists to be with him — the leader of the poor — or to be his enemies, allied with the oligarchy. Journalists' democratic opposition to Bucaram was based on their rejection of his antipolitics based on mass-entertainment. Instead of shifting public opinion in his favor, Bucaram lost his war against the media. As a representative of a marginal economic and political elite, Bucaram could not control or neutralize the privately-owned media. His vulgarity antagonized the sectors who write opinion pieces and who are interviewed by the media. As a result he was overthrown, and the media constructed him and continues to present him as the embodiment of all the country's ills.

In contrast to Bucaram, Rafael Correa defeated the media. He stayed in power for ten years, changed the constitution, got rid of the old parties, created laws and institutions to control the content of what the media could publish, economically strangled critical media venues, and created a government-run media conglomerate. The state took over ownership of the two most popular television stations and a newspaper.

In a country without a distinction between the state and government, Correa used these media venues to broadcast his voice as the only truth. In addition, he used mandatory television and radio broadcasts to advertise his policies, public works, his speeches in international forums and, of course, to attack critics.

The main innovation of Correa's media strategy was the weekly radio and television program *Enlace Ciudadano* (Citizen's Connection or Citizen's Ties), which were broadcast for about two hours every Saturday morning. Between 2007 and 2017, 523 *Enlaces* were broadcast adding up to 1,346 hours. The president became a charismatic figure, the "center of the nation," who irradiated his power to the margins. Power became materialized in the president's words. He became the professor of the nation when he pedagogically explained his policies. More pragmatically, he set the weekly news agenda.

His television and radio shows allowed Correa to enter into direct contact with the people. The day before, the president and his cabinet met with local authorities and organized free cultural acts where they brought musicians. By visiting remote regions that politicians and state officials rarely visited, he reinforced his charisma. Like the Kings discussed by Clifford Geertz, Correa visited all the nation's territory trying to become the center of the social order.

Enlace Ciudadano followed the same ritual. Correa sat at a podium from which, like an old-time college professor, he lectured to the nation. He used power point presentations to explain policies. In one *enlace*, for example, he explained in detail a project for pharmaceutical industries to develop generic medicines, the new law of sports, and the need for the state to get higher royalties from oil companies. The public nodded and responded with a yes or a no to the questions that he asked his audience. There was rarely a dialogue between citizens and their president. At most he invited one of his ministers to explain a particular law or policy, but the impression was that Correa was knowledgeable on all topics, and that he was the one in charge. These interactions illustrated how power worked in his regime: the president-professor of the nation lectured to a public who could acclaim him, but who did not have the opportunity to engage in critical dialogues.

His performances illustrated that he was the embodiment of the nation and of the state. He took notice of the beauties of his homeland and of the delicacies of local regional cuisine. He said: "I who had the opportunity to travel abroad can assure you that Ecuador is the most beautiful country of the world." In a town on the Coast he manifested "even humpback whales come to Ecuador to make love." He also talked about his private life, his dreams and personal accomplishments. After delivering lectures at Oxford and at the London School of Economics, he explained how important those academic institutions are. On another occasion he narrated how, during a family trip to the Pichincha volcano, they spotted a fox.

To show that he was like the common people, he used colloquial popular language. He told that he came from a humble social background, but was superior to the common man because he studied abroad on scholarships, getting a Ph.D. in economics at the University of Illinois, Urbana. This is why he could master technocratic and scientific language. In addition, he joked, sang, and asked the public to chant slogans against the opposition with him. When he referred to what he labeled as the "barbarities" of the opposition and the private media, he raised his tone of voice and got red with anger.

The most commented segment of his TV and radio show was entitled "freedom of expression belongs to all of us" (*la libertad de expresión ya es de todos*), clearly referring to the slogan used by his administration "the homeland now belongs to all of us" (*la patria ya es de todos*). He said that the bourgeois press is the new opium of the people. He used the lyrics of Argentinean protest singer Piero, which said: "everyday, and all the time, newspapers published trash." He also used the lyrics of Víctor Heredia: "they lied, they always lied." Politics was hence transformed into a personal dispute between his persona, who tells the truth, and the lies of the mass media. He characterized journalists and journalism as "*mafiosos*, journalistic pornography, human wretchedness, savage beasts, and idiots who publish trash." He sued journalists and newspaper owners, claiming that editorial pieces and investigative reports on corruption had caused him moral harm. He closed over twenty radio stations, a major newspaper was pushed to bankruptcy, and the best journalists migrated to the web.

Whereas Bucaram's attempt to transform politics into media spectacles was read as the eruption of barbarism and vulgarity, Correa was able to use the media to represent himself and have legitimacy as a technopopulist. On his TV shows, he performed the roles of the populist that attacks enemies and of the technocrat with the answers and prescriptions to lead his country to hyper-modernity. Correa put experts in charge of his administration. These technocrats under his leadership dreamt about transforming an oil-producing and agro-export country into a producer of biotechnology and nanotechnology. Because of the grandiosity of their project, they needed to broadcast their achievements without the interference of journalists who asked difficult questions.

Controlling and Regulating the Media

The elections of Silvio Berlusconi and Thaksin Shinawatra showed that ownership of the media could lead populists to power. The former made his fortune in cable television and is the owner of three of the seven major television stations. The latter had a telecommunication empire that included cable television, satellites, television stations and Thailand's biggest mobile company. Once in power, Berlusconi interfered with the independence of the national broadcaster Radiotelevisione Italiana (RAI) and Thaksin Shinawatra intruded on election coverage, instructing television stations to cut down on negative news. Moffitt explains, "Thaksin pursued a number of defamation cases, and even opinion pollsters were harassed and intimidated."

Populism has a difficult relationship with liberal-progressive conceptions of democratic communication. Silvio Waisbord writes in his chapter in *The Routledge Handbook of Global Populism* that this model is grounded:

"in the existence of the public commons (that includes public, private and mixed, legacy and digital media), that facilitates and promotes informed public dialogue characterized by civility, diversity, tolerance, reason, and facts. This model historically entailed the guarantee of constitutional rights and institutional settings to catalyze news and public debate."

Populists as diverse as Donald Trump, Viktor Orbán, Rafael Correa and Michael Sata have embarked on wars against the media. These leaders devalue truth and the practices of professional journalism. Whereas Orbán and Trump favor particular private media venues, control and regulation of the media by the state was at the center of the leftist populist struggle for hegemony. Chávez and Correa enacted laws to regulate the content of what the media could publish; the state took away radio and television frequencies from critics. The state became the main communicator in these nations. Their governments used and abused mandatory broadcasts that all media venues were forced to air, and created their own TV shows, *Aló Presidente* and *Enlaces Ciudadanos*. Every Sunday, Chávez addressed the nation for four to six hours, and Correa talked every Saturday. They set the informational agenda as they announced major policies on TV shows where they also sang popular tunes, talked about their personal life and dreams, and viciously attacked opponents and journalists. Chávez and Correa became ever-present figures in the daily life of Venezuelans and Ecuadoreans. They were always talking on the radio and on television, and citizens became polarized by deepening divisions between loyal followers and enemies.

Populists are media innovators and use old and new media to establish direct links with their followers, bypassing political parties. Perhaps the Five Star Movement made the most creative use of the new media. In his chapter in *The Routledge Handbook of Global Populism*, Benjamin Moffitt shows how Grillo launched a blog in 2005 to call his supporters "to organize offline local meetings through the meetup.com platform. These culminated in large events entitled 'V-Day' in 2007 and 2008, and the Five Star Movement (M5S) was officially launched in 2009." The M5S's "political rhetoric has revolved heavily around messages of cyber-utopianism and the democratic promise of the web."

The logics of the media and populism are complementary and explain some of the shifts of politics into entertainment, the proliferation of populist media outlets, and the closure of spaces for pluralistic debates. Populist media venues are used as channels for international diffusion. Online publications like *Breitbart News* or the British *Westmonster* have become forums for right-wing European and American pundits and politicians to exchange views. Transnational left-wing populist groups like DiEM25, headed by the former Greek Minister of Finance Yanis Varoufakis, use the new media to speak for "we, the peoples of Europe." Chávez and other Latin American presidents of ALBA launched teleSUR as an alternative to U.S.-dominated media like CNN.

Chapter 4

The Promises
and Perils of Populism
for Democracy

Populisms have different effects on democracies that
are going through their first process of democratic
incorporation as compared to democracies with
established party systems. Parliamentary systems
tend to de-radicalize populists in power, whereas
the chances of populist ruptures are higher in
presidentialist systems. This chapter is divided into five
sections. The first discusses the simultaneous process
of inclusion and closure of spaces to the opposition
during the first wave of populism in Latin America
and with Michael Sata in Zambia. The second studies
populist critiques of democracies where citizens

were incorporated into parties. The following section analyzes processes of socioeconomic inclusion and simultaneous democratic erosion in Venezuela, Bolivia and Ecuador. The fourth analyzes how the populist playbook eroded Hungarian democracy, and speculates about the future of American democracy under Trump. The last section briefly compares different populist successions.

Inclusion and Autocracy during the First Incorporation into the Political System

Populism in Latin America emerged in the 1930s and 40s with the crisis of the oligarchic social order, which combined liberal-inspired constitutions (division of powers and elections) with patrimonial practices and values. Everyday practices of domination excluded the majority of the population from politics and the public sphere. Populist leaders and their followers rebelled against electoral fraud, and fought for the expansion of the franchise. They also challenged everyday practices of domination, marginalization and stigmatization. Populists were famous for turning the stigmas of the people into virtues. Historian Natalia Milanesio explains how, in the 1930s and 40s, the elites of Buenos Aires used the term *"cabecita negra"* to refer to the "dark skin and black hair" of internal migrants. They racialized Perón's followers as "black Peronists" or as "greasers," evoking not only the dirt and oil on worker's overalls but all that is cheap or in bad taste. Juan and Eva Perón transformed the shirtless masses despised by the elites into the embodiment of the Argentinean nation. Eva, for instance, used "the term *grasita* to affectionately refer to the poor." The despised mob became the "beloved rabble" of the Colombian populist Jorge Eliecer Gaitán, and of José María Velasco Ibarra in Ecuador.

In Latin America, populists privileged a notion of democracy based more on the quasi-liturgical incorporation of common people through mass rallies than on the institutionalization of popular participation through the rule of law. Herbert Braun shows how Jorge Eliécer Gaitán in his unsuccessful bid for the presidency in 1945 mobilized the masses, altering "the face of politics and public life" in Colombia. His followers paralyzed traffic with torchlight processions, organized motorcades through the central streets during rush hour, and after the grand finale of the campaign when an enormous multitude attended Gaitán's speech in the Circo de Santamaría bullring, the crowds marched through Bogotá chanting: "In the Circo of Santamaría, the oligarchy has died."

Peronism was experienced as an exceptional moment, when working-class crowds took over public spaces from which they were previously marginalized. Workers mobilized on October 17, 1945, to demand the liberation of general Perón. They marched from the outlying areas to the central plazas. Elites and the middle-classes saw their presence as the irruption of barbarism, of the *cabecitas negras* (the dark-skinned) in places reserved for the high society (*gente bien*). By invading the public plazas — spaces where citizens gather and political power resides — the workers from outlying areas challenged the spatial hierarchy, affirming their right to belong to the public sphere.

Historian Daniel James argues that Perón extended the notion of democracy from political rights "to include participation in the social and economic life of the nation." Perón's source of legitimacy lied in winning open and free elections. Peronism expanded the franchise, voter turnout, and women won the right to vote. Historian Mariano Plotkin writes that real wages increased by 40% between 1946 and 1949.

Perón's model of populist democracy, while inclusionary, was at odds with notions of accountability, the division of powers, and bypassed mechanisms of checks and balances. Enrique Peruzzotti reports in his chapter in *Latin American Populism in the Twenty-First Century* that after winning his first democratic election in 1946, Perón declared: "we have given the people the opportunity to choose, in the cleanest election in the history of Argentina, between us and our opponents. The people have elected us, so the problem is resolved. What we want is now done in the Republic of Argentina."

By 1950, after reforming the constitution to allow for Perón's reelection, all institutions of government were in Peronist hands. Perón replaced the members of the Supreme Court with staunch defenders of his regime, and had firm control over Congress and the Senate. Historian Luis Alberto Romero writes in his *History of Argentina*, "at every level of government, all power was concentrated in the hands of the executive — whether mayor, governor, or president — making it clear that the movement and the nation were considered one." Perón accused members of the opposition in Congress of contempt, barred them from the chamber of deputies, and even stripped some representatives of their congressional immunity. In the elections of 1951, Peronists won all the senate seats and 90% of the chamber of deputy seats.

Perón temporarily closed critical media outlets and expropriated newspapers such as *La Prensa* and *La Nueva Provincia*. His government created a chain of radio stations and newspapers. According to Mariano Plotkin in his book *Mañana es San Perón*, the *Subsecretaría de Prensa y Difusión* "published more than 2.5 million pamphlets of various types and more than 3 million posters, in addition to producing movies and other propaganda materials." Perón dominated the labor movement by displacing and jailing communist, socialist and anarchist leaders, and by promoting cronies to the leadership of the powerful national labor confederation, CGT.

His educational policies sought to expand access to previously excluded groups, and simultaneously to create Peronist national subjects. Mariano Plotkin reports that the number of high school students rose from 38,686 in 1946 to 46,942 in 1951, and the number of students at the University of Buenos Aires increased from 17,742 in 1941 to 41,325 in 1951. Women's illiteracy was reduced from 15% in 1947 to 9.38% in 1958, while the proportion of women college graduates increased from 15.67% in 1946 to 24.15% in 1955-60. In a speech delivered in 1953, Perón "defined himself as the first indoctrinator of the nation who 'delegates to the Argentinean teachers and professors the responsibility of inculcating [the Peronist doctrine] in the children and youth of the New Argentina.'" Textbooks were Peronized. Eva's autobiography became mandatory reading at all levels of education. Federico Finchelstein reports in *The Ideological Origins of the Dirty War* that children learned to read and write their first words with sentences such as Evita loves me, or Perón loves children.

Juan and Eva Perón were erected into mythical and even religious-like figures. The author of *The Ideological Origins of the Dirty War* writes that Evita asserted: "Perón is a God," while other Peronists professed that "God is Peronist." Eva Perón herself was portrayed as a saint: "She was the First Samaritan, the Lady of Hope, and just before her death, she became the Spiritual Leader of the Nation."

With the closure of democratic institutions to voice dissent, the streets became the main venue to show loyalty or opposition to Perón. His movement was born with spontaneous worker demonstrations that demanded his liberation from jail on October 17, 1945. The government used demonstrations to cement loyalty to Perón, and the opposition took to the streets against him. In October 1954, university students went on strike against Perón nationwide and hundreds of students were arrested.

In the early 1950s, Perón entered into conflicts with the Catholic Church over his educational policies, the construction of Evita as a saint after her death and the formation of the Christian Democratic Party as an oppositional force to Peronism. In May 1955, Perón proposed a constitutional amendment to separate the church from the state. Perón's followers and the Church clashed in the streets. In June, 100,000 middle-class protesters marched through the streets of downtown Buenos Aires. Several days later, thousands of Peronist workers gathered for a counterdemonstration in the Plaza de Mayo, the city's main square, and burned churches. On June 16, 1955, the navy and opposition politicians staged a failed coup that resulted in the death of 300 civilians. Finally, Perón was ousted in September. The military governments that succeeded him were much more repressive. Perón was banned from returning to Argentina until 1973. He died in power in 1974, and his widow Isabel was overthrown by a brutal military junta in 1976.

Zambia transitioned to democracy in the early 1990s. The Movement for Multi-party Democracy

(MMD) dominated politics. Michael Sata formed the Patriotic Front to challenge the power of the MMD and to rectify the economic marginalization of the majorities who made a living in the informal sector of the economy, while also appealing to previously marginalized ethno-linguistic groups like the Bembas. Danielle Resnick in her contribution to *The Promise and Perils of Populism* explains, "urban inequality as measured by the Gini coefficient, is estimated at 0.66 and poverty levels in the capital of Lusaka approximated 48 percent by 2004." Approximately 69% of the population worked in the informal sector, and in Lusaka 70% of the population lived in shantytowns. In contrast to other politicians who launched their campaigns from fancy hotels or in major conference facilities, Sata held rallies in shantytowns and launched his 2008 campaign in the Matero market.

8. The famous Plaza de Mayo in Buenos Aires (Argentina), recurrent setting for the affirmation of rights.

His nickname was "King Cobra" due to his ferocious attacks on his opponents. Alastair Fraser in his article "Post-populism in Zambia" explains that Sata's "brazen rudeness about his opponents was central to his charismatic appeal. He communicated one message: Your anger at those in power is legitimate; I share it." In the 2006 campaign, his supporters in Lusaka asserted their right to the street by staging rallies, demonstrations and riots. In contrast to his opponent, who commissioned jingles and posters, Sata used popular songs and his supporters had self-made banners. In a rally in Lusaka in 2011, Resnick reports, Sata exclaimed, "You liberated yourselves from Europeans, how can you fail to liberate from Rupiah [the leader of the MMD]? There is no water in schools and there are pit latrines. How can you use pit latrines 47 years after independence." Sata promised: "to upgrade rather than demolish shantytowns, provide a clean water supply, and cease harassment of street vendors." Simultaneously, he appealed to ethnic identities in the Northern and Luapula provinces where his co-ethnics, the Bemba, live. He won the 2011 elections with the support of urban centers and ethnic rural votes. He ruled until his death in 2014.

President Sata ordered local government officials to stop harassing street vendors, doubled the royalties of mining companies, passed minimum wage legislation and led a plan to build roads. Yet, as in other populisms, inclusion was not matched with pluralist practices and respect for the rule of law. Daniel Resnick shows how Sata used elections as plebiscites on his rule and was anti-pluralist, even jailing Hakainde Hichilema, the leader of an opposition party, on the dubious grounds that he defamed the president. He used the judiciary for his personal political objectives, made use of defamation lawsuits against independent media outlets, controlled NGOs, and transformed government officials and the rank and file of his own party into sycophants who tried to show greater loyalty than their colleagues. Sata increased voter turnout and addressed some of the socioeconomic demands of the poor, yet simultaneously disdained political institutions and civil liberties, in the end undermining democratic institutions.

The first incorporation into the political community under populism had a record of addressing some socioeconomic demands of the poor, and of expanding the franchise. Yet their disrespect for the rule of law and closure of spaces to opponents led to the erosion of pluralism. When the opposition felt totally marginalized from democratic institutions, they plotted coups. The history of Argentina, Brazil, Peru, Ecuador, Panama and Thailand under the Shinawatras was characterized by cycles of populist government followed by a military coup.

Populist Promises to Redeem Decaying Party Democracies

Hugo Chávez, Rafael Correa and Evo Morales got to power after widespread intellectual critiques and popular rebellions against neoliberalism and restricted democracies. Left-wing and Christian Democrat intellectuals in Venezuela debated about how to improve democracy by complementing liberal models with participatory institutions. During his first years in office, Chávez's project was to create participatory institutions to improve the deficits of liberal democracy. As explained in Chapter 3, most of these participatory experiments depended on Chávez's directions. Nonetheless, the poor used these opportunities to push for their demands. After Chávez decided to change his program to Socialism of the Twenty-First Century, he sought to replace bourgeois with socialist democracy. In Chávez's words, socialist communal democracy would transcend representative liberal democracy with the "real and quotidian exercise of power by the great majority of common people."

Even though he never militated in a leftist party, nor was a fervent reader of Marx and Marxism, Rafael Correa adopted their critique of formal democracy as the rule of the bourgeoisie, promising to replace it with real democracy based on equity and the redistribution of wealth. He was also influenced by the anti-party feelings of many Ecuadorians who demanded on the streets to get rid of corrupt politicians who followed the policies of the IMF, disregarding national sovereignty.

Bolivian indigenous intellectuals like Silvia Rivera Cusicanqui, Félix Patzi and Esteban Ticona have articulated the most intriguing and creative critique of liberal democracy. They distinguish indigenous communal direct democracy from liberal democracy. They argue that indigenous communal democracy is a form of direct and unmediated democracy where all members participate and deliberate until they reach a consensus and a decision is made. Participation is not reduced to voting and to the delegation of power to representatives. Leadership is considered a duty and it rotates among community members. Representatives are accountable to their constituents and have to implement what has been decided by the collective. Those who dissent and do not follow collective decisions can be punished with monetary fines, ostracism and sometimes even by means of physical penalties. Individual rights are subordinated to collective rights. Felix Patzi writes, "in indigenous communities democratic rules do not apply, but a form of authoritarianism based on consensus." Community assemblies, he argues, are undifferentiated institutional spaces where decisions are made, justice is administered and where authority is constructed.

The demands for real and authentic direct democracy to replace representative models are not confined to Latin America. Charles Lindholm and Pedro Zúquete show in their volume *The Struggle for the World* how direct democracy is a demand of the New European right and of right-wing European populists. "They ardently hope to establish a pure form of popular sovereignty that will pit the immediate will of the disfranchised people against the overwhelming power of the global elites. Articulating this perspective, Le Pen declared, 'I, and only I, incarnate democracy'."

Mabel Berezin in *Illiberal Politics in Neoliberal Times* shows how the National Front (now National Rally) was transformed from an anti-Marxist, racist and xenophobic party into the party against globalization, Europeanization, multiculturalism and globalist political elites. She also argues that the issues of the National Front (NF) became French issues, and that moderate right wing parties adopted some NF demands. "Le Pen's anti-Europe and anti-globalization rhetoric gave voice to a national mood that lacked a public forum." In the process, the French accepted the message while rejecting the extreme xenophobic messenger. After the NF entered into a period of dédiabolisation, it was ideologically successful in pushing demands against Europeanization and globalization to the mainstream. This also led to the political failures of Jean Marie Le Pen. His daughter, Marine, continued with the process of de-demonization, abandoning anti-Semitism, homophobia and sexism, recasting Islam as a threat to Western civilization, and expelling her father from the party. Marine's National Rally claims to defend women and gay rights from Islamic men, demonized as threats to Muslim women and to Western culture and civilization. It is a new xenophobia dressed up as defense of the project of the Enlightenment from which Muslims are excluded with essentialist criteria based on old Orientalist stereotypes.

Representative Democracy: a Failed Attempt

The failures of representative democracy to live up to its promises to give power to the people make populist critiques credible and repetitive. Perhaps in Europe they also resonate because when democracies were reestablished after Nazism and fascism, political elites sought to restrict appeals to popular sovereignty. Jan-Werner Müller in *Contesting Democracy* argues that "Western Europeans fashioned a highly constrained form of democracy, deeply imprinted with a distrust of popular sovereignty — in fact, even distrust of traditional parliamentary sovereignty." Parliaments were weakened and constitutional courts empowered to protect the new order and safeguard individual rights.

European integration was part of the new constitutional ethos, and "European Community law had supremacy over national laws." Politics became a technocratic endeavor because "there really were technically correct solutions to social and economic problems; it simply made no sense to keep fighting about them." Müller argues that a democracy modeled on Schumpeter as competition for votes among elites was created. The rest of democratic ideology was considered to be an illusion, and politics "was not supposed to be a source of meaning at all."

Restricted technocratic democracies were challenged for surrendering national sovereignty to transnational institutions. Whereas the National Front used nationalist and xenophobic tropes to resist globalization and Europeanization, left populists like Podemos and Syriza do not use anti-immigrant rhetoric. These left parties challenged the technocratic consensus of austerity policies from the established parties. They rebelled against massive youth unemployment of 60% in Greece and 40% in Spain. They politicized the rage of massive protest movements against austerity and the technocratic arguments that led to the imposition of painful austerity policies. They demanded a real democracy, and used a discourse of the people against the caste or the oligarchy. Even though the leadership of these parties established a series of participatory platforms and claimed that their view of the people is open for contestation, there are conflicts between charismatic leaders who seek to impose their points of view and the more horizontal sectors in these parties. Critics are warning that Syriza and Podemos are becoming more leader-centric, less horizontal and more vertical, and that Tsipras and Iglesias are attempting to become the only rightful voice of the people. For instance, John Judis writes that after winning a referendum with 62% of the vote against new austerity policies of the Troika, "Tsipras astonished Greek voters and many in his own party by returning to the talks and agreeing to terms that were more onerous than the Troika had demanded earlier."

9. Election posters from the Politicians for Syriza campaign, January 28, 2015, Athens (Greece): Portrait of Alexis Tsipras and the slogan "Hope is on the way."

Populism in Power

To disentangle the effects of populist regimes on democracy, it is useful to differentiate how they promote or restrict citizenship rights while in power. This section differentiates how the administrations of Chávez, Morales and Correa implemented political, socio-economic, civil, collective, and gender and sexuality rights. Whereas their records on political and socioeconomic rights are positive, they are negative on civil rights, in particular the rights of association and communication. Collective, gender and LGTBQ rights were included in constitutions, but were implemented unevenly.

Citizenship as Active Political Participation

Populism is a model of citizenship conceived as the active participation of the people in politics. Chávez, Morales and Correa used three strategies to engage the active participation of their citizens: regime change by constitution-making, permanent elections and campaigns, and establishing institutions for participatory democracy at the local level.

Constitution-making became the utopia for the construction of a more participatory and equal society, and the strategy to change the institutional framework of society. Constitution-making would refound the state to make it more inclusive, and would establish a true democracy. The processes to draft the new constitutions in these nations were participatory and involved social movements. The new Venezuelan, Bolivian and Ecuadorian constitutions were approved in referenda. These constitutions expanded rights and established a different kind of democracy based on elections and also on a new constitutional order that concentrated power in the hands of the president.

Populist presidents convened numerous elections to consolidate their power and to create new hegemonic blocks. Venezuelans voted in 16 elections between 1999 and 2012, Bolivians in 9 between 2005 and 2016, and Ecuadorians in 11 between 2006 and 2014. All these elections were plebiscitary referenda on their presidents. By constantly campaigning, populist presidents kept their charismatic links with their constituencies alive. They relentlessly traveled around their countries, had an overwhelming presence in the media, and distributed resources to followers and potential voters.

Populist citizenship was thus lived as an antagonistic struggle against internal and external enemies. Populist polarization and emotional discourses on behalf of the poor, exalted as the soul of the nation, created strong popular identities. These identities allowed for the mobilization of common people in mass rallies, demonstrations, and in elections where they voted for their leaders. Populist followers had the feeling of being actors and shapers of their own political destinies. They were struggling against their oppressors and for their own liberation.

Populist polarization, however, transformed rivals into enemies, restricted spaces for dialogue and compromise, and reduced democracy to the plebiscitary acclamations of leaders. In contrast to the liberal model of citizenship that protected pluralism, populists conceived "the people" as an organic and homogenous whole that shared one interest and identity that could be embodied in a leader.

Populist Socioeconomic Rights

Left-wing populists understood socioeconomic citizenship as the reversal of neoliberal models of citizenship as consumption based on the individual's capacity in the market. In contrast to the neoliberal model based on the privatization of social services, reduction of the size of the state and decentralization, they enacted policies that strengthened the state and its role in the economy as the main engine of growth. They used the state to reduce inequalities, redistribute wealth, and to increase the consumption of the poor in the market.

Venezuela, Bolivia and Ecuador were rich in hydrocarbons and reaped huge benefits from the commodity boom of the 2000s that sent oil and natural gas prices to record levels. As a result of enhanced revenues, public investment and social spending skyrocketed and poverty rates and, to a lesser extent, inequality fell. World Bank figures indicate that the poverty rate fell from 55.4% of the population in 2002 to 28.5% in 2009 in Venezuela. Poverty in Ecuador was reduced from 37% in 2006 to 29% in 2011. In Bolivia it dropped from 60% in 2006 to 50.6% in 2009, with an even greater decrease in levels of extreme poverty. Falling oil prices led to an increase of poverty in Venezuela. According to the Economic Commission for Latin America, it jumped from 24% in 2012 to 32% in 2013. Another study concluded that 75% of Venezuelans were poor according to their income in 2015.

10. Wood homes in a poor neighborhood in Caracas, Venezuela.

Despite their rhetoric of changing the economic matrix of natural resource exploitation and oil and mineral rents, these governments increased state spending without altering the structural dependencies on minerals of their economies. The percentage of Venezuela's export earnings derived from oil increased from 68.7% in 1998 to 96% in 2016. In Bolivia, the exports of extractives rose from 41.8% in 2001 to 74% in 2009. In Ecuador, oil exports increased from 41% in 2002 to 58% in 2011, and Ecuador opened its doors to large-scale mining interests.

In addition to readdressing the consumption deficits of the poor, populists sought to give them access to the symbols of status regularly enjoyed by the middle-class. Chávez, for example, launched the "Great Housing Mission" during his 2012 presidential campaign. His objective was not only to solve housing deficits; it was also to give the poor access to houses of middle-class status in modern apartment complexes similar to those where the middle-class live. His housing mission was complemented with the Mission "*Mi Casa Bien Equipada*" that sold household appliances at subsidized prices to the poor. The message was that Chávez's government was providing consumer goods associated with middle-class status to the very poor.

The expansion of consumption and new lines of credit undoubtedly contributed to the popularity of Bolivarian presidents. Yet prosperity lasted as long as the boom of the economic cycle, and the economic crises provoked by the collapse of commodity prices could lead to resentment among the recently incorporated consumers, who might lose their feeble middle-class status as fast as they attained it.

Restriction of Civil Rights and the Colonization of Civil Society

Vast literature has shown that civil rights were not always respected in Latin American democracies. Rights were selectively enforced, and in many nations there was a duality between the enshrinement of civil rights in constitutions and in official discourse, and the limited upholding of these rights in everyday life. The rule of law was tenuous at best, and at worst the law appeared to serve the interests of the powerful few. Getúlio Vargas's famous maxim "for my friends everything, for my enemies the law!" continues to characterize the selective enforcement of civil rights in the region.

The innovation of Bolivarian leaders was to transform the historical patterns of selectively enforcing laws into tools to secure their hold on power by punishing critics. Chávez, Morales and Correa transformed Vargas's old maxim into policies that Kurt Weyland in "The Threat From The Populist Left" called "discriminatory legalism." He defines this term as the use of formal legal authority in discretionary ways. New laws were created in these nations to restrict civil liberties such as the rights of free information and freedom of association. In the name of upholding the law, citizens were deprived of their rights, as when protest was criminalized and opposition politicians and social movement leaders were charged with terrorism and sabotage. These governments abused the law, such as when the legal system was used to impose astronomical fees on journalists and owners of privately-owned media. Laws were not always enforced, like when electoral boards allowed incumbents to use state resources in their political campaigns.

In order to use laws discretionarily, populist presidents packed the courts and institutions of accountability with loyal followers. After drafting the new constitution, the Venezuelan Assembly created a transitory council that governed legislative affairs between the approval of the constitution in December 1999 and the election of the new congress in August 2000. By controlling this council, Chávez put trustworthy authorities in charge of the National Electoral Council. In 2004, Chávez put the highest judicial authority, the Supreme Tribunal of Justice, in the hands of loyal judges. By 2006, hundreds of lower court judges were fired and replaced by unconditional supporters. Correa followed Chávez's model of convening a transitory council after the assembly drafted the new constitution. The "congresillo" was tasked with naming the new judicial authorities and the people in charge of the institutions of accountability, such as the ombudsman and the comptroller. In 2011, Correa created an ad hoc *Consejo de la Judicatura* charged with appointing the members of the National Court, the highest judicial authority. Gustavo Jalkh, who was Correa's personal secretary, was named head of the *Consejo*. Similarly,

Morales gained control of the Supreme Electoral Tribunal. Between 2006 and 2009, his administration dismantled the Supreme Court and the Constitutional Tribunal, gaining control of the courts after 2010.

Populists argued that the private media acted as an opposition political party. Morales, for example, on several occasions said that the media was his "number one enemy." Control and regulation of the media by the state was at the center of the populist struggle for hegemony. Chávez led the path in enacting laws to control the privately-owned media. In 2000, the Organic Law of Telecommunication allowed the government to suspend or revoke broadcasting concessions to private outlets when it was "convenient for the interest of the nation." The Law of Social Responsibility of 2004 banned "the broadcasting of material that could promote hatred and violence." These laws were ambiguous, and the government could interpret their content according to its interests. Correa's government emulated Chávez. In 2013, the National Assembly controlled by his party approved a communication law that created a state institution tasked with monitoring and regulating the content of what the media could publish. The Superintendence of Communication SUPERCOM initiated 269 processes against journalists and private media outlets. Most of these processes resulted in sanctions that included fines, written warnings, public apologies and rectification of previous statements. In Bolivia, a well-intentioned yet vaguely drafted law against racial discrimination in the media was used to intimidate the private media.

To challenge the power of the private media, Chávez's government used discriminatory legalism and took away radio and television frequencies from critics. The state became the main communicator, controlling 64% of television channels. In Bolivia, media concessions were equally divided between the state, the private sector, and popular and indigenous organizations. Correa created a state media conglomerate.

Chávez and Correa suffocated the private media by reducing government advertisements on critical media venues and by manipulating the subsidies for the price of paper. They used discriminatory legalism to intimidate and harass journalists and private media owners. Correa sued the owners of newspapers and journalists who uncovered cases of corruption or were critical to his administration. The most notorious cases that were reported worldwide involved an editor and three board members of the largest privately-owned newspaper, *El Universo*, who were convicted of defamation and sentenced to three-year terms for publishing an editorial entitled, "No to Lies"; the paper was also fined US$40 million. Subsequently, president Correa pardoned them.

Bolivarian presidents enacted legislation that used ambiguous language to control and regulate the work of non-governmental organizations (NGOs). In 2010, the Law for the Defense of Political Sovereignty and National Self-Determination in Venezuela barred non-governmental organizations that defended political rights or monitored the performance of public bodies from receiving international assistance. Three years later, in 2013, Correa enacted Executive Decree 16. This decree gave the government authority to sanction NGOs for deviating from the objectives for which they were constituted, for engaging in politics, and for interfering in public policies in a way that contravenes internal and external security or disturbs public peace. To set an example, the teacher's union and the environmental organization Pachama Alliance were closed for deviating from the original organization's goals, and for interfering with public policy and security. Morales followed suit by passing legislation in 2013 to revoke an organization's permit to operate if it performs activities different from those listed in its statutes, or if the organization's representative is criminally sanctioned for carrying out activities that undermine security or public order.

In Bolivia and Ecuador, the right to participate was restricted to groups that were recognized and authorized by the state. In Venezuela and Ecuador, social movements were created from the top down to counteract the power of workers' unions, unionized teachers, students and indigenous groups. At the same time, these organizations distributed resources to loyal followers that promoted the interest of their governments. Protest was criminalized in these nations. Union leaders and striking workers, even when they were sympathizers of Chávez, were charged with terrorism. Hundreds of peasant and indigenous activists were accused of terrorism and sabotage in Ecuador. Laws were used discretionally to arrest and harass leading figures of the opposition in the Bolivarian nations. The most notorious cases occurred under Nicolás Maduro. Opposition leader Leopoldo López faced time in jail on trumped up charges of inciting violence.

By incrementally reducing civil rights, by using the state to regulate the media and civil society, and by harassing the opposition, the governments of Venezuela, Bolivia and Ecuador slowly killed democracy. The adoption of ideas and models of revolution were at the heart of these processes of democratic erosion. Bolivarian leaders understood politics as a struggle of friend versus enemy a la Carl Schmitt. Instead of facing democratic rivals, they confronted real or imaginary national and foreign enemies. Traditional political parties, the owners of the privately-owned media, the leaders of social movements, NGOs, journalists and some economic elites were attacked as enemies of the revolution. The closure of spaces for contestation and the rhetoric of revolutionary confrontation cornered the opposition, whereas power was concentrated in the hands of the presidency.

These leaders were convinced that they were leading long-lasting revolutionary transformations; therefore, they could not be limited by "bourgeois formalities" such as term limits. Chávez's example of modifying the constitution enacted during his presidency to stay indefinitely in power inspired Correa to change the constitution and do away with term limits, as well. However, to not rule in a conjuncture of economic crises and when his popularity rate dropped, he opted to not participate in the 2017 election and used the power of the state to put Lenín Moreno in the presidency. Morales lost a referendum in 2016 that would have allowed him to run for yet another term, but will modify the constitution to run again in 2019.

The Ambiguities of Cultural, Collective, Gender and LGBTQ Rights

Deborah Yashar wrote that Indigenous and Afro-descendant movements that emerged in the last third of the twentieth century demanded a reconfiguration of citizenship that entailed: "1) constitutional recognition that national identities coincided with ethnic and racial ones; 2) legal recognition that there should be multiple units of political representation, including individual citizens and ethnic communities; and 3) legal pluralism, respecting national and indigenous jurisdiction and jurisprudence — including the right to territorial autonomy." They demanded cultural rights to language, traditions and ways of life, and collective rights to territory and autonomous self-government.

The constitution of 1999 recognized the multicultural nature of Venezuela and the rights of indigenous people. Three indigenous representatives were allocated to the unicameral national assembly, and larger percentages were assigned to local and provincial bodies according to the percentage of indigenous people. Interestingly, Afro-Venezuelans who comprise a larger proportion of the population were not granted collective rights

Bolivia was declared plurinational and communitarian in the constitution of 2009. The constitution equates autonomy with self-governance, and asserts recognition of the 36 indigenous languages as official languages of the state. It recognized representative, participatory and indigenous communal democracy. Despite the promise to complement liberal with indigenous communal democracy, the institutions for indigenous democracy and collective rights have not been firmly established. For example, even though indigenous representatives were elected in indigenous territories, they were not chosen following the practices of indigenous communal democracy. Indigenous representatives were elected through the mechanisms of representative democracy. The state also limited the implementation of collective rights to territorial self-government when it stated that consultation to exploit natural resources in indigenous territories was not binding. Anthropologist Nancy Postero writes that the

Morales administration "sees indigenous control over natural resource extraction as a threat to its own power."

11. Group of Bolivian women wearing their traditional dress during the May 1 parade in La Paz, Bolivia.

Indigenous and Afro-Ecuadorean cultural rights to language, traditions and ways of life were recognized in the Constitution of 1998. The new Charter of 2008, drafted with the participation of social movements, expanded cultural rights and set limits on collective rights to territory and self-government. The constitution recognized plurinationalism, but Anthropologist Carmen Martínez Novo writes that "Special representation of indigenous nationalities beyond regular democratic representation was not accepted." Indigenous territories were recognized, but the process of establishing these territories became difficult to implement. Even though the constitution established that indigenous people should be consulted on whether to exploit natural resources located in their territories, this consultation was not binding.

Participatory constitution-making gave activists opportunities to promote gender and, to a lesser extent, LGBTQ rights. The 1999 constitution and legislation passed by the Chávez administration banned discrimination and domestic violence, gave pensions to housewives, and gave breastfeeding protection. The Bolivian constitution banned discrimination based on sex, gender identity, sexual orientation, color and pregnancy, and recognized sexual and reproductive rights as constitutional rights. The Ecuadorian constitution included an antidiscrimination clause on the basis of gender identity as well as sexual orientation.

How Populist Policies Benefited Women

Populist presidents included women in visible positions in the public sphere, and used gender quotas in the election of representatives. Their redistributive policies benefited women. Chávez, for example, created the state's women's bank, and promoted missions that targeted women. Yet despite gains, there were many contradictions and problems in fulfilling feminist and especially LGBTQ agendas. Javier Corrales writes that whereas Venezuela under Chávez and Maduro, and Morales's Bolivia, did not move forward in recognizing LGBTQ rights, these rights – with the exception of marriage and adoption – were recognized in Correa's Ecuador. Constitutional gains for LGBTQ rights were ambiguous at best. For instance, the Ecuadorian constitution, while at the same time changing the traditional view of the family and recognizing nonkinship-based households, stipulated that only a man and a woman could get married. President Correa, a practicing Catholic, voiced his opposition to same sex marriage, to abortion which continues to be illegal, and even attacked gender studies saying: "a gender ideology that fails under any academic analysis."

The dominant view of womanhood in the Bolivarian revolutions was motherhood. Chávez appealed to women as mothers and nurturers. Morales, for his part, privileged the role of women as mothers, combatants and activists for social change, putting leaders of women peasant unions in symbolically important positions. Amy Lind in "Contradictions that Endure: Family Norms, Social Reproduction, and Rafael Correa's Citizen Revolution in Ecuador" writes that for Correa his revolution "has a woman's face," implying that "women as mothers and caretakers would be the political and reproductive foundation of the new socialist nation." These traditional constructs of womanhood as maternity, Espina and Rakowski argued in their chapter in *Gender and Populism in Latin America*, "honors and reinforces both women's traditional roles as self-sacrificing mothers and wives and their unpaid work as volunteers in their communities."

Radical populists thus had an ambiguous legacy on citizenship and democratization. While their socioeconomic policies redistributed income and wealth, they did not break their nation's dependency on natural resource extraction. Hence, their inclusionary policies were not sustainable in the medium-term. Even though they promoted the active participation of followers, participation took place under the guidance of the leader. More troublesome adversaries became enemies, and these leaders reduced rights to information and association. Civil rights were selectively enforced, and the legal system was used in novel ways to punish critics and favor cronies. Indigenous, Afro-descendants, women and LGBTQ organizations used the openings in participatory constitution-making to push some legislation on their behalf. Yet communal rights were constrained by the deepening of natural resource extraction, and gender and LGBTQ rights were limited by the conservative beliefs and prejudices of populist presidents.

The Populist Playbook

Populists in Latin America, Hungary, Turkey and the U.S. followed a similar playbook: reducing the independence of powers and concentrating power in the presidency, wars against the media, control of civil society, colonization of state institutions by loyal followers and discriminatory legalism to punish critics. Viktor Orbán followed the populist playbook by eroding a well-functioning democracy from within. Aron Buzogány in his article "Illiberal democracy in Hungary" explains:

> "Post-communist Hungary was considered a success story of democratic consolidation. It featured a stable party system and strong governments; it was the leading country in the region in attracting foreign direct investments (FDI) and eventually became one of the front runners being considered for European Union (EU) membership."

Orbán's party Fidesz won the 2010 election and secured a two-thirds majority in congress. Orbán was elected after eight years of incompetent and corrupt Socialist rule. Once in office, he set about a project to transform Hungary into what he described in a speech in 2014 as an illiberal new state based on national foundations. The government purposely marginalizes opposition forces by weakening existing state institutions (including the courts) and creating new, largely autonomous governing bodies and packing them with Fidesz loyalists. His party transformed the civil service law, Müller writes, "to enable the party to place loyalists in what should have been nonpartisan bureaucratic positions." He weakened checks and balances on executive power, and adopted a majoritarian electoral system by redesigning electoral rules to make it difficult for the fragmented opposition to mount an effective challenge. Fidesz has won all national and European Parliament elections since 2010 with big margins. His administration created a regulatory body to control the content of what the media could publish. Agnes Batory in "Populists in Government" reports that "Fidesz loyalists directly or indirectly acquired the ownership of important media outlets, and government appointees dominated the management of public service broadcasters, leaving little space for unbiased political discourse." Orbán confronted and discredited NGOs, accusing them of being controlled by foreign powers and serving external interests. His administration, according to political scientist Agnes Batory, displaced democracy to "the gray zone between liberal democracy and fully blown authoritarianism."

In contrast to Latin America, democracy in the U.S. was not in crises. Even though citizens distrusted parties and traditional politicians, the institutional framework of democracy was robust. The Constitution separates governance between three branches of government, breaks up representation over time and space, divides sovereignty between the national government and the states, and filters political expression into two parties. Under these institutional constraints, it is difficult to find majoritarian control of government as in Latin America, and until Trump's election populism was confined to the margins of the political system. Perhaps populist movements are ultimately unsustainable in America's liberal democracy. Joseph Lowndes writes, "Homogeneous notions of the people and the transparency of representation between the people and its leaders in a large, diverse and modern society is no more than a fantasy of wholeness." Trump's populism under this hypothesis would be no more than a passing nightmare, and the institutional framework of U.S. democracy and civil society would be strong enough to process populist challenges without major destabilizing consequences. Weyland and Madrid in "Liberal Democracy Stronger than Trump's Populism" forcibly concluded: democracy in the United States will prove resilient because Trump did not get to power during a crisis, and due to the strength of liberal institutions.

An alternative and plausible scenario is that Trump, who came to the presidency when the executive had more power over the legislative, with the Senate and Congress in the hands of Republicans, with the power to name ultra-conservatives to the Supreme Court and to lower courts, could attempt to follow the Latin American and Hungarian populist playbook of controlling all the institutions of the state. He put loyalists in key positions of power. He threatened Republicans who did not support him wholeheartedly, and it is not inconceivable that he might want to transform the Republican Party —a party to which he does not have any long-lasting loyalty— into his personalist venue.

Like other populists, Trump does not like the media. At his rallies, he led his followers to heckle journalists who were placed in a separate section. He threatened to use libel, and menaced to sue newspapers. He said, "The Rolling Stone magazine should be put out of business," and threatened to sue *The New York Times.* Christopher Caldwell reported in *The New York Times* that during the campaign "journalists who opposed Mr. Trump received photos of themselves —and in some cases their children —dead, or in gas chambers. Jewish and Jewish-surnamed journalists were particular targets." After assuming power, Trump embarked on a war against the media. He has argued that the media is a political machine that aims to harm his policies on behalf of the American people. He tweeted that the New York Times, NBC, ABC, CBS and CNN are the "enemy of the American people."

Trump used coarse language against civil rights groups like Black Lives Matter, and even African-American athletes who protested against police brutality. His policies of mass deportations, stop and frisk in poor and predominantly Black and Latino neighborhoods, surveillance of American Muslims, and rolling back gender and LGBTQ rights would lead to confrontations with civil and human rights organizations.

Even if the institutional framework of democracy does not collapse under Trump, he has already damaged the democratic public sphere. Hate speech and the denigration of minorities are replacing the politics of cultural recognition and tolerance built by the struggles of feminists and anti-racist social movements since the 1960s. Trump's potential incremental attacks on civil liberties and human rights, confrontations with the media, use of the legal system to silence critics, has disfigured and eroded democracy.

The Perils of Populist Succession

Populist successions are often problematic, if not catastrophic. On the one hand, like other politicians whose legitimacy lies in wining free elections, populists see the vote as the only legitimate tool to name and remove presidents. But on the other, in contrast to democrats who view the office of the president as disembodied and distinguish holding an office temporarily from owning it, populists attempt to stay in power until achieving their mission of liberating their people. They use elections, but voting takes place in skewed fields that blatantly favor incumbents, do not give guarantees to the opposition, and constrain pluralism under the assumption that the populist leader is the only truthful voice of the people and that enemies are constantly conspiring.

Until the third wave of democratization, populists were frequently removed by military coups. Yet once the international community viewed elections as the only legitimate tool to remove leaders, coups became costly and presidents were often removed by impeachments. Populists Fernando Collor and Abdalá Bucaram, for example, were impeached in the 1990s. Coups unfortunately are still used. Thaksin Shinawatra in Thailand and Manuel Zelaya in Honduras were toppled by the military.

As in the past, right-wing populists like Alberto Fujimori or leftist populists such as Hugo Chávez or Rafael Correa made it difficult to have peaceful democratic successions, and tried to stay in power until liberating their people. Hugo Chávez changed the constitution enacted by his coalition to be reelected for as many times as he could. However, cancer took his life. Without Chávez's charisma and in a context of profound economic and social crises, Nicolás Maduro's power base is the military and Venezuela is no longer a democracy. Maduro used cronyism, repression and widespread corruption to keep his coalition united.

In 2000, after Fujimori seemed to have surmounted the problem of legitimacy in his second fraudulent reelection, his government unexpectedly collapsed. He ruptured with his chief of intelligence, Vladimiro Montesinos, over his advisor's involvement in a network of military corruption that sold weapons to the Revolutionary Armed Forces of Colombia (FARC). Despite appearing to be all-powerful, Fujimori was weak because he never built a real political party, nor was he interested in promoting popular organizations. The unexpected collapse of Fujimori's autocratic regime opened up possibilities to reinstate democracy in Peru. Valentín Paniagua, who served as president of the congress, was sworn in after Fujimori sent his resignation letter from Japan. Paniagua led the re-democratization of Peru by respecting the independence of the different branches of the state, following the rules of the democratic game, and allowing for freedom of expression and association. Fujimorism, however, did not vanish with its leader. Despite Fujimori serving terms in jail for human rights abuses and corruption, his family took over his movement preserving a base of support of about 20%, and his daughter Keiko was close to winning the presidency in 2011 and 2016.

When populists are not able to displace democracy towards competitive authoritarianism, as in Argentina under Nestor and Cristina Kirchner, the Peronist Party lost an election and peacefully transferred power. Mauricio Macri won the runoff elections in 2015 with a slim margin of less than 2%. Yet in the parliamentary elections of 2017 his coalition won the election, even defeating Cristina Kirchner in the Province of Buenos Aires. Macri broadened his base of support from the middle-class to the lower middle-class and used clientelism to appeal to the poor. The Peronists divided between a radical faction that followed Cristina and a more pragmatic sector under Sergio Massa. However, at the time of writing this book in September 2018, with the collapse of the Argentinean peso it was unclear if Macri would be able to successfully finish his term in office in a nation where all non-Peronist presidencies have been interrupted.

Another path of transition occurs when the populist coalition disintegrates, as in Ecuador. Lenín Moreno, Correa's hand-picked candidate, won the 2017 elections in Ecuador. Surprising friends and foes alike, Moreno broke with him. Jorge Glass, who served as Correa's vice-president and briefly under Moreno, and several of Correa's top officials are in jail for corruption. Moreno won a referendum in February 2018 to end Correa's prospects for permanent re-election, and to dismantle Correa's control of all the institutions of accountability and of the judicial system. Rafael Correa has an order of preventive prison on him for failing to appear to testify in the case of the failed kidnapping attempt on Ecuadorian politician Fernando Balda in Colombia. Moreno is moving Correa's competitive authoritarian regime towards an electoral democracy. The government is not at war with the media, is letting civil society organizations function without fear of repression, and has given independence to the institutions in charge of justice and accountability. The rule of law is returning. Still, as in any transition from autocracy,

Ecuadorians will have to wait until the 2019 and 2021 elections to evaluate if Moreno will allow them to take place on even playing fields, respecting the rights of the opposition and the fairness of elections.

Legitimacy of Populist Leaders

The uncertainties of populist transition are explained by populism's dual source of legitimacy: elections and a Messianic leader. In his book *From Fascism to Populism*, historian Federico Finchelstein argues that populism became a different "ism" when it accepted elections as the only legitimate mechanism to get to power. In contrast to fascists, who disdained elections and all institutions of liberal democracy as impediments for the people to express its will, populists adapted to democratic times. Yet at the same time, the populist leader was constructed by followers and viewed himself or herself not as a regular politician, but as the chosen one to lead the liberation of their people. Because of the immensity of his historical task, the leader was not bound by the rules of the democratic game that constrain regular and normal politicians, such as term limits and alternation of power. Perón wanted to rule for 60 years; Chávez and Correa changed the constitution to have the option of being reelected forever.

Populist leaders are constructed as extraordinary figures and as saviors of their nations. The name of the leader becomes synonymous with their projects for transformation. They built personalist movements that could facilitate their ascension to power, and this becomes the main obstacle to building long-lasting projects. Yet the effects of populism on democratization depended, as shown in this chapter, on whether the population was politically included in parties or not; whether they were presidentialist or parliamentary regimes; the type of crises of political representation; the density of civil society; and the strength of national and supranational democratic institutions.

Historical experiences contradict the optimistic assertions of left-wing populist advocates of "aspirational populism," or as the Laclaunian answer to democratize depoliticized systems ruled by technocrats. As shown in this chapter, despite promises to enact more participatory models of democracy, populism ended in competitive authoritarian regimes in Venezuela, Bolivia and Ecuador. Similarly, Marcus Mietzner, an expert on populism in Asia, after reviewing in detail Narendra Modi's national populism in India, Thaksin Shinawatra in Thailand, Joko Widodo in Indonesia and Rodrigo Duterte in the Philippines, wrote in his chapter in *The Routledge Handbook of Global Populism*, "in Asia, there has been no case of a populist who improved the quality of democratic participation, civil liberties, and other indicators of democracy's health." Dani Filc in his contribution to *The Routledge Handbook of Global Populism* also showed how, in Israel and Turkey, societies characterized by ethno-conflicts, populism led to further exclusion of ethnic and religious minorities.

Conclusions

Populisms. A Quick Immersion first of all shows the diversities of populism worldwide. Some use ethnicity, while others build upon political and socioeconomic criteria to construct the people. Pierre Rosanvallon writes that "the people," like Janus, has two faces: "it menaces the political order at the same time that it grounds it." The concept of the people is still used, as in earlier times, to refer to the threat of dangerous mobs that could be mobilized by demagogues. Other scholars and activists challenge these images of the perilous masses by constructing the people as inherently virtuous and legitimate. As Margaret Canovan writes in *The People*, they imagine the people as a "mythic being that is not only the source of political legitimacy, but can sometimes appear to redeem politics from oppression, corruption, and banality." Theories of populism oscillate between these poles: for some populism is a threat to democracy, civility and even to the project of the Enlightenment, whereas for others it would renew democracy.

In *Politics at the Edges of Liberalism*, Benjamín Arditi urges us to not speak of populism in general when analyzing its relationship with democracy. Following his suggestion, light and full-blown populism should be differentiated. By light populism, I refer to political parties and politicians that occasionally use populist tropes and discourses, but that do not aim to rupture existing institutions. Under this criteria, Bernie Sanders, who did not break with the Democratic Party creating a third party, is a light populist. Similarly, when Ignacio Lula da Silva used anti-oligarchic rhetoric, he was a light populist. Full-blown populists aim to rupture existing institutions by polarizing society and the polity into two camps of enemies, and constructing a leader as the symbol of all demands for change and renewal. Light populists are almost indistinguishable from other politicians in contemporary democracies, who appeal to trust in their personas and use the mass media to bypass traditional parties. Full-blown populists often use democratic institutional mechanisms and mass collective action to try to bring change. When seeking power, full-blown populists appeal to constituencies that the elites despise or ignore, using discourses and performances to shock and disturb the limits of the permissible and to confront conventions. Does it mean that all populist challenges to constituted power are favorable to democratization? How to distinguish between populist appeals that favor or counter democracy?

For Laclau, his followers and Laura Grattan, the answer is straightforward: let's build aspirational, left and democratic forms of populism. Right-wing appeals to xenophobia, racism and colonial nostalgia are considered, with very good reasons, to be unacceptable. Ethnic and religious constructions of the people with essentialist cultural or racial categories, they rightly argue, could lead to processes of exclusion and de-democratization. They propose constructing the people as those that are dispossessed by political and economic arrangements and demand a deepening of democracy. These theorists, as well as the political parties that have used Laclau's theory, claim that left-wing constructs of the people are open for contestation, plural and indeterminate. Yet as the experiences of Podemos, Syriza and the MAS in Bolivia show, there are tensions between leaders who pretend to be the only voice of the people and their constituencies, who do not surrender to the voice of the leader. Charismatic leaders lead these parties. Pablo Iglesias even proudly claimed that his name represented Laclau's empty signifier, the nodal point of the chain of equivalence against Spanish restricted and neoliberal democracy.

Populists of all colors posed two main perils to plural and democratic polities: the transformation of rivals into enemies, and their subordination to a charismatic leader. Unfortunately for those who defend populism, in order for a movement to be effective in conquering political power a leader is needed, otherwise populists remain at the margins. To create strong identities that could lead to mobilizations and mass action, populists must build enemies. Given how populisms right and left try to appropriate the voice of the people, it is surprising how some leftists continue to view these movements as aspirational. In order to have horizontal democratizing movements that innovate democratic practices and discourses, a leader is not needed. And when anarchist or horizontal democratic practices were linked to populist vertically strong leaderships, the end result was that the anarchists were absorbed or displaced by the populist.

If all strong or full-blown populisms are potentially dangerous to democracy, its results ultimately depend on institutional and historical conditions. Parliamentary systems often forced populists into pacts and agreements, and thus to de-radicalize their claims. After Podemos entered into a coalition with the PSOE in 2018 to get rid of the conservatives in power, it became like Syriza a few years before, part of the establishment. Despite their rhetorical claims of rupture, Syriza and Podemos are becoming conventional parties that nonetheless present demands that other parties have not articulated. They are not a threat to democracy, and Greece under Syriza has not experienced processes of democratic erosion. Yet parliamentary systems are not immune to populist challenges, and could succumb to populist majoritarianism, as in Hungary under Orbán. By controlling parliament, the courts, and aggressively following a populist playbook, he displaced democracy to the gray zone of hybridism. Stronger civil societies and democratic institutions did not allow Nestor and Cristina Kirchner to bring about a populist rupture in Argentina. Populist ruptures occurred in presidentialist systems when all the institutions of democracy, such as parties, congress, the judiciary and the media, lost legitimacy. Under these institutional and historical settings, despite their democratizing promises, the governments of Chávez, Correa and Morales displaced democracies in crisis to the gray zone of hybrid regimes.

To avoid empiricist arguments that populism is both a threat and a corrective to democracy, there is a need for normative groundings to distinguish populist critiques from their solutions, and to differentiate between demands that could enhance from those that would restrict democracy. Demands that aim to further democratize plural and democratic civil societies and public spheres should be taken into consideration and debated. For example, the loss of national sovereignty to supranational institutions, the reduction of citizens to consumers, the technocratic depoliticization of democracies, the lack of responsiveness of political elites, increasing social inequalities brought on by globalization, and the control of the media by monopolies are important issues to correct deficits of participation, representation and legitimacy. However, if solutions are based on the transformation of rivals into enemies, and in assuming that only one sector of the population is the real and authentic people, populist answers are simplistic and ultimately perilous for democracy. Populist anti-pluralist demands should be rejected. That is why appeals to essentialist notions of ethnicity, culture and religion are more often than not dangerous. Their aim is to restrict democracy just to those who fit into these constructs.

Regardless of how they build the category of the people, and of whether populists are left, right or beyond these distinctions, all populist demands follow a *pars pro toto* dynamic. Populists exclude those that 1) do not accept the leadership of a self-proclaimed Messiah and his acolytes, and 2) the parts of the population that are excluded from the legitimate people on religious, ethnic, cultural, political or socioeconomic criteria. Hence all populists, even those who claim to include the part that plays no part, the poorest of the poor or the downtrodden, exclude those individuals and organizations from the oppressed sectors of society that do not accept the wisdom of the leader.

Populists thrive in democratic and plural civil societies where they form organizations, media venues and political parties. Yet their views are contrary to pluralism and often to democracy. They do not forge relationships with other organizations, and despise those who do not follow their leader as traitors to the people and the nation. Civil society is also one of the most important sites of resistance to populism. Those who value pluralism, who aim to make democracy more inclusive, participatory and receptive to the demands of different constituencies, have organized in civil society against populist processes of democratic erosion. Because populists do not abolish all democratic institutions, they leave spaces open for dissent, and civil society is one of the main arenas to challenge autocrats. Rafael Correa was prevented from seeking a fourth term in office, even after changing the constitution, by massive demonstrations. Trump's presidency was met with massive protests defending women rights, migrants, science, and demanding gun control.

In a context where the international community no longer accepts coups as tools to remove presidents, populism is becoming, in Enrique Peruzzotti's apt words, "democracy's nemesis." As shown in previous chapters, in the name of improving democracy and returning power to the people, populists targeted checks and balances, the principle of separation of powers, the role of the opposition, of a critical press and of autonomous organizations in civil society. Populist regimes are based on elections, yet elections are viewed as plebiscites to confirm the leader's power and authority. As Peruzzotti argues, populism in government and as a regime "is likely to promote a specific path to regime change, one consisting of the gradual hybridization of the structure of liberal democracy through the selective removal of some of the latter's defining features."

Hence for many intellectuals and activists, the question of what should be done with populism is becoming urgent. Some propose to contain populists.

Writing in the *Oxford Handbook of Populism*, Stefan Rummens, who has in mind extreme right-wingers in Europe, wrote: populists "should be relatively free to operate in the informal public sphere of the periphery of the democratic system, but tolerance for these forces should decrease as they come closer to the actual centers of power." Chantal Mouffe disagrees, showing how a cordon sanitaire failed in Austria, for example, because it transformed politics into morality. She claims that to counter the power of xenophobic populism, the left has to create alternative emancipatory populisms. Yet Latin American experiences with left populists in power should give caution to idealizations of left populism. Perhaps the answer lies in addressing some of the populist demands in democratic and pluralist ways. The left should be wary of creating populist Frankensteins, and falling into Schmittian constructs of rivals as enemies. In order to improve democracy, there is no need to forge a liberator who would later devour his acolytes and even a plural population in the name of a mythical people. Institutions that allow for plural civil societies and public spheres, and that enhance the division of power and the rule of law, should not be undermined. However, real existing democracies are not panaceas. Democratization is a process, and constituent power under conditions of plurality and of not surrendering power to a Messiah could enhance democracy.

Populisms: a Quick Immersion shows the need to analyze populism in its global connections. Perón and

Chávez sought to export their models of political and social change. With an abundance of petrodollars, Chávez created supranational institutions to counter U.S. hegemony: the ALBA and teleSUR. ALBA was not a regular commercial treaty between nations. It was rather a political alliance, and a learning space where populist presidents, their cabinets, advisors and social movement leaders who supported these governments met to exchange information and to learn from each other. Chávez provided a utopia of social transformation and a strategy to achieve change. Under his leadership, the project of socialism returned to political debates. This time it became a third way between failed neoliberal and Communist projects. It aimed for a third path of development under strong state control of the economy and society. It sought to restrict the privileges of the rich and to redistribute resources and opportunities to the poor. Chávez also offered a new revolutionary strategy. Instead of using bullets, he used ballots to bring a revolutionary transformation of politics, the economy, civil society and culture. Still, twenty-first century socialism, instead of deepening democracy, eroded it and, under Nicolás Maduro, led to autocracy.

Right-wing European populist parties regularly convene at the Europe of Freedom and Direct Democracy in the European Parliament. Donald Trump invited several right-wing European populists to his inauguration, and he is an inspiration for right-wing European leaders, and to Bolsonaro.

Geert Wilders considered that Trump's election was a "revolution," and Marine Le Pen talked about the "emergence of a new world." As Federico Finchelstein wrote, Washington is becoming the new center for diffusion of right-wing populism. According to the *Huffpost*, Steve Bannon, Trump's short-lived strategist, set up a Brussels-based foundation called *The Movement* to conduct polling, messaging, data targeting and think-tank research for far-right politicians across Europe. Whether he is successful or not, what is important to keep in mind is that the new nationalist and populist parties in Europe and beyond have strong transnational links, and they learn from each other.

12. Poster in a bar in El Salvador supporting Hugo Chávez. With varying levels of success, Chávez promoted presidential candidates in Peru, Nicaragua, Bolivia, Mexico and Ecuador.

This short volume looks at global populism from Latin American experiences because that is the region where populists have governed since the 1930s and 40s. Peronism and Chavism are considered by all theorists to be the paradigmatic cases of populism, and it could be argued that Perón was the first to develop what I have described as the populist playbook. What lessons can the anti-populist opposition in other world areas learn from Latin America? First and fundamentally, that military interventions against populist autocrats failed even when they were successful in the short-term. After Perón was overthrown and exiled in 1956 and his party was banned, democracy became an impossible game in Argentina. The failed coup against Chávez radicalized his project, and only when the Venezuelan opposition followed the electoral road did they become serious contestants. Even so, the opposition could not stop Maduro from consolidating an autocratic regime based on the military, cronyism and widespread corruption.

Second, the media in Latin America played a role in allowing populists to become the center of their nations. Their obsession with sales and rankings, and their transformation of news into entertainment played well with populists in power. Willingly or not, they allowed populists to become the main media event and the center of the social order. Washington Post journalist Margaret Sullivan wrote that the journalistic mission of holding the powerful accountable "remains crucially important. Maybe more than ever." Journalists worldwide are often at the vanguard of resistance to populist autocrats, and they are also often one of the main targets of populist rage. Democratic citizens need to support critical media outlets and be vigilant against attacks on journalists and the debasing of journalistic professionalism.

Third, civil society became the main site of worldwide resistance to populist autocrats. Organized citizens marched against autocratic policies, and organizations favorable to populist leaders often pushed for their own agendas. Plural civil societies resisted the populist attempt to transform the people into a homogeneous whole incarnated in a politician. The politics of civil society under populism are based on massively taking the streets to protest, and on civil disobedience. Even though populists thrive on polarization, it can become a weapon of resistance when it is used by a plurality of actors and organizations to resist autocrats. As N. Turkuler Isiksel argued in an article published in *Dissent Magazine* in November 2016, "the only democratic, nonviolent practice capable of deterring the autocrats is the sight of endless crowds marching: vociferous, tenacious, disciplined citizens claiming ownership of their constitutional liberties and defending the integrity of their political institutions."

Populisms, even when they fail, will not disappear. They are the specter of democracy, as Benjamín Arditi puts it. Populists will politicize polities where citizens are transformed into consumers. Populists will rise up against inequalities, and in nations where the laws are used to punish the poor and to favor the rich. Populists will emerge against corruption and the grip of unresponsive politicians. However, democrats and progressives have to be wary of being seduced by populism. The lessons of populists in power, even those that promised more democracy and inclusion, is one of displacing democracy towards hybrid regimes. The transformation of rivals into enemies, of a politician into the people's avatar, and the *pars pro toto* dynamic are certainly dangerous to the politics of plural civil societies and public spheres. Hopefully, the left will not be seduced by populism, and will focus on creating pluralities of associations and groups to resist populism and to push for the further democratization of real existing democracies.

Further Reading

Anselmi, Manuel (2018). *Populism: An Introduction.* Routledge: New York.

Arato, Andrew (2013). *Political Theology and Populism.* Johns Hopkins University Press: Baltimore. Social Research 80 (1): 143-172.

Arato, Andrew; Cohen, Jean L. (2017). *Civil society, populism and religion.* Constellations (24): 283-295.

Arditi, Benjamín (2007). *Politics on the Edges of Liberalism: Difference, Populism, Revolution, Agitation.* Edinburgh University Press: Edinburgh.

Berezin, Mabel (2009). *Illiberal Politics in Neoliberal Times. Culture, Security and Populism in the New Europe.* Cambridge University Press: Cambridge.

de la Torre, Carlos (2010). *Populist Seduction in Latin America.* 2 ed. Ohio University Press: Ohio.

de la Torre, Carlos; Arnson, Cynthia J. (Eds) (2013). *Latin American Populism in the Twenty-First Century.* The Woodrow Wilson Center Press and the Johns Hopkins University Press: Washington and Baltimore.

de la Torre, Carlos. (Ed.) (2015). *The Promise and Perils of Populism: Global Perspectives.* The University

Press of Kentucky: Lexington.

de la Torre, Carlos. (Ed.) (Forthcoming). *The Routledge Handbook of Global Populism*. Routledge: New York.

Errejón, Iñigo; Mouffe, Chantal (2015). *Construir Pueblo. Hegemonía y Radicalización de la Democracia*. Icaria: Madrid.

Filc, Dani (2015). *Latin American Inclusive and European Exclusionary Populism: Colonialism as an Explanation*. Journal of Political Ideologies 20 (3): 263–283.

Finchelstein, Federico (2017). *From Fascism to Populism in History*. University of California Press: Oakland, California.

Garrido, Marco (2017). *Why the poor support populism: The Politics of Sincerity in Metro Manila*. American Journal of Sociology 123 (3): 647-685.

Germani, Gino (1978). *Authoritarianism, Fascism, and National Populism*. Transaction Books: New Brunswick, New Jersey.

Hawkins, Kirk A. (2010). *Venezuela's Chavismo and Populism in Comparative Perspective*. Cambridge University Press: Cambridge.

Hofstadter, Richard (1955). *The Age of Reform*. Alfred A. Knopf: New York.

Horwitz, Robert B. (2013). *America's Right. Anti-Establishment Conservatism from Goldwater to the Tea Party*. Polity Press: Cambridge.

Judis, John B. (2016). *The Populist Explosion. How the Great Recession Transformed American and European Politics*. Columbia Global Reports: New York.

Laclau, Ernesto (1977). *Politics and Ideology in Marxist Theory*. Verso: London.

Laclau, Ernesto (2005). *On Populist Reason*. Verso: London and New York.

Levitsky, Steven; Loxton, James (2013). *Populism and competitive authoritarianism in the Andes*. Democratization 20 (1): 107–136.

Lindholm, Charles; Zúquete, José Pedro (2010). *The Struggle for the World: Liberation Movements for the 21st Century*. Stanford University Press: Stanford, California.

Madrid, Raúl L. (2012). *The Rise of Ethnic Politics in Latin America*. Cambridge University Press: Cambridge.

Moffitt, Benjamin (2016). *The Global Rise of Populism: Performance, Political Style, and Representation*. Stanford University Press: Stanford, California.

Mudde, Cas; Kaltwasser, Cristóbal Rovira (2012). *Populism in Europe and the Americas*. Cambridge University Press: Cambridge.

Mudde, Cas; Kaltwasser, Cristóbal Rovira (2017). *Populism: A Very Short Introduction*. Oxford University Press: New York.

Müller, Jan Werner (2016). *What Is Populism?* University of Pennsylvania Press: Philadelphia, Pennsylvania.

Peruzzotti, Enrique (2017). *Populism as Democratization's Nemesis: The Politics of Regime Hybridization*. Chinese Political Science Review 2 (3): 314-327.

Roberts, Kenneth M. (2014). *Changing Course in Latin America: Party Systems in the Neoliberal Era*. Cambridge University Press: Cambridge.

Kaltwasser, Cristóbal Rovira; Taggart, Paul; Ochoa Espejo, Paulina; Ostiguy, Pierre (2017). *The Oxford Handbook of Populism*. Oxford University Press: Oxford.

Ruzza, Carlo; Fella, Stefano (2009). *Re-inventing the Italian Right. Territorial Politics, Populism and 'Post-Fascism'*. Routledge: London and New York.

Skocpol, Theda; Williamson, Vanessa (2012). *The Tea Party and the Remaking of Republican Conservatism*. Oxford University Press: Oxford.

Urbinati, Nadia (2014). *Democracy Disfigured: Opinion, Truth, and the People*. Harvard University Press: Cambridge, Massachusetts.

Waisbord, Silvio (2013). *Vox Populista: Medios, Periodismo, Democracia*. Gedisa: Buenos Aires.

Weyland, Kurt (2001). *Clarifying a Contested Concept*. Comparative Politics, 34 (1): 1–22.

Zúquete, José Pedro (2007). *Missionary Politics in Contemporary Europe*. Syracuse University Press: Syracuse, New York.

Available soon:

Happiness
Ben Radcliff & Amitava Krishna Butt

Human Rights
Peter Rosenblum

French Revolution
Jay Smith

Global Waste
Anne Berg

Federalism
John Kincaid